AF130777

Sabrina Hoeling

Can R2P practice what it promises?

A Case Study on the Syrian Civil War

Anchor Academic
Publishing

Hoeling, Sabrina: Can R2P practice what it promises? A Case Study on the Syrian Civil War, Hamburg, Anchor Academic Publishing 2015

Buch-ISBN: 978-3-95489-357-7
PDF-eBook-ISBN: 978-3-95489-857-2
Druck/Herstellung: Anchor Academic Publishing, Hamburg, 2015

Bibliografische Information der Deutschen Nationalbibliothek:
Die Deutsche Nationalbibliothek verzeichnet diese Publikation in der Deutschen Nationalbibliografie; detaillierte bibliografische Daten sind im Internet über http://dnb.d-nb.de abrufbar.

Bibliographical Information of the German National Library:
The German National Library lists this publication in the German National Bibliography. Detailed bibliographic data can be found at: http://dnb.d-nb.de

© Anchor Academic Publishing, Imprint der Diplomica Verlag GmbH
Hermannstal 119k, 22119 Hamburg
http://www.diplomica-verlag.de, Hamburg 2015
Printed in Germany

Acknowledgements

As every other project this book is not the sole product of my own determination and ability. Many people helped by contributing with their expertise on the topic such as all the academics I met at several conferences and most importantly my supervisor Dr. Reem Abou-El-Fadl, with whom I enjoyed discussing my dissertation and whose meetings I always left more motivated and full of new ideas. However, it was also the emotional support that helped to reach my goal. Hereby, I thank you all: first of all my parents who have always believed in me, and my brother Sven who has, sometimes intentionally, at other times unintentionally, appealed to my ambition to write about a topic nobody dared to write about and to give my best.

Secondly, I thank my dear friends Nicole, Kim and Pippa who were so patient to read my dissertation and were very honest in giving feedback. Especially Pippa went over it several times and her comments helped me to improve constantly. Every student and university will be glad to have you three.

Thirdly and lastly, I am so grateful for all the friends I made during my time in Durham, my Amigos who actually seemed to enjoy listening to my progress, or non-progress, every Wednesday night and even though they sometimes could not understand what I was talking about always said that I was working on an interesting topic; and of course my dear friends Magda and Alex with whom I worked side by side in the library for hours and who provided me with chocolate and tea. Without all of you guys, this would never have made it into a book. Finally, you have a chance to read the result of my hard work. Enjoy!

Table of Content

List of Abbreviations

EU	European Union
FSA	Free Syrian Army
GA	General Assembly of the United Nations
ICC	International Criminal Court
ICISS	International Commission on Intervention and State Sovereignty
ICRtoP	International Coalition for the Responsibility to Protect
IHL	International Humanitarian Law
ISIS	Islamic State of Iraq and Syria
R2P	Responsibility to Protect
NATO	North Atlantic Treaty Organisation
NGO	Non-governmental organisation
UK	United Kingdom
UN	United Nations
UNHCR	United Nations Human Rights Council
UNSC	United Nations Security Council
US	United States
WSOD	World Summit Outcome Document

1   Introduction

"Since the Holocaust we have been required to treat others as we treat
ourselves [...] we are responsible for the other who looks at us, faces us,
who raises claims on us. We are responsible not for everyone, but
everyone who is within our reach [...]. If we do not recognize our humanity
in others we will not recognize it in ourselves" (Cooker, 2001: 148f).

With these words, Cooker (2001) summarises the development of moral theory and
international human rights in the last decades, a trend which indicates that we are all part of
an international community with a responsibility both towards our compatriots and towards
strangers. As a result, the Responsibility to Protect (R2P) doctrine was born, which was
adopted by the United Nations (UN) as part of its commitment to protect human rights
worldwide. However, the debate about R2P has been ongoing ever since, with academics
and politicians experiencing difficulties in agreeing on at which point state sovereignty can
be overridden for the protection of human rights (Welsh, 2011; Schütte, 2012).

This debate has its origin in the divided English school where pluralists, such as Bull (1977),
believe in the integrity of states and the principle of state sovereignty, whereas solidarists,
such as Fabre (2012) and Buzan (2004), argue in favour of a promotion of human rights over
non-intervention. Subsequently, the emerging literature on the theoretical concept of R2P
and its implementation can be divided into two main categories: the first group of scholars
are R2P critics who argue that R2P is mainly concerned with humanitarian interventions and
is thus likely to be abused by western states trying to dominate weaker countries (Ayoob,
2004; Hehir, 2010). In addition, they defend state sovereignty as an unalterable principle of
the international system which should never be overridden since R2P, with its new
perception of sovereignty, self-determination and humanitarian interventions, only

increases insecurity within the international system (Mason and Wheeler, 1999; Mamdami, 2010). In contrast, the second group of scholars are in favour of the concept: Bellamy (2009) disputes the fact that the traditional understanding of sovereignty, as is understood by R2P critics, "bears [...] resemblance to contemporary world politics" (p.60). Instead, he argues that each state today is to some degree accountable to the international community: by joining international institutions such as the UN, and thereby accepting some restrictions on how to rule within state borders, sovereigns have already restrained their absolute power (ibid; Stahn, 2007). Furthermore, the second group of scholars criticises that R2P has not been implemented sufficiently in international law, and that more R2P ultimately leads to a just international society (Welsh, 2004; Wheeler, 2000).

The first humanitarian intervention under R2P in Libya in 2011 fuelled the debate regarding R2P's mechanisms and the assumed hidden interests of global players, even though R2P advocates celebrated it as a triumph since the humanitarian intervention resulted in an end to the civil war, and thus saved the lives of thousands of Libyans. The current Syrian civil war, in which sexual violence, chemical weapons, torture, and killings of civilians are known to be war strategies by all conflict parties, has led to calls for an intervention on behalf of the Syrian civilians in the western media and by non-governmental human rights organisations.

So, why has the UN failed to intervene in Syria, as it did in the Libyan conflict? It would seem that the international community does not to react according to a responsibility for the Syrian civilians, even though the severity of human rights abuse exceeds the one in Libya. Does the United Nations Security Council (UNSC) have valid reasons to not pass a resolution legitimising a joint military intervention by UN members? That is, does the Syrian case not fall within R2P, or are state interests responsible for preventing the UN from finding an international consensus on how to help the Syrian population?

While the aforementioned theoretical literature on R2P might provide arguments for a discussion about the relevance of the principles of state sovereignty versus the commitment to respect human rights and punish severe human rights abuse, it fails to compare the legal and political implementation of R2P with its practice. Legal scholars, such as Stahn (2007), concentrate on the legal implementation and implication of R2P in international law, whereas moral theorists, such as Bellamy (2009) and Weiss (2004), focus on the normative aspects. Despite the fact that both groups of scholars refer to the other's research field, there is no work which thoroughly investigates all aspects of R2P. In addition, academic literature on the current situation in Syria is rare and mostly analyses the conflicts in the context of the Arab Spring but not in the context of human rights violation, even though it is the scale of atrocities which set Syria apart from other Arab countries (Gause, 2011; Hinnebusch, 2012; Goldstein and Western, 2013; Ajami, 2012).

Consequently, the main objective of this study is to examine the theoretical implications of the UN's responsibility to protect and apply these to a practical case. Syria is particularly interesting to investigate since the Syrian civil war has been persisting since 2011 and even though there is evidence that the scale of violence and suffering in Syria is extreme, with over 160,000 deaths up to this point, and millions of Syrians fleeing from mass atrocities to neighbour countries (Human Rights Watch, 2014), the international community has been unable to end it.

This dissertation firstly postulates that the humanitarian emergency in Syria indeed falls within the scope of R2P, and secondly that the UN has not exhausted all of its available instruments to prevent this conflict from escalating into a civil war with mass atrocities and to react to the existing considerable human rights abuse. Thirdly, it asserts that the Syrian case is an example of the practical ineffectiveness of R2P, and that state interests still prevail over the responsibility to protect strangers.

It is beyond the scope of this study to give a comprehensive analysis of R2P, but rather this work will attempt to contribute to a better understanding of R2P in practice by highlighting the weaknesses and strengths of a norm in its implementation. In other words, this dissertation will assess R2P in a new light and will thus bridge the deficit in R2P literature. It is hoped that the value of this study will bring attention to the need to do more research on how well the international community's commitment to certain norms fares when put to the test, and to continue the search for an international consensus on how to effectively protect human beings from mass atrocities.

1.1   Methods and Sources

In order to find out whether R2P practices what it promises, this dissertation will use triangulation to compensate for the weaknesses of a single method by "counterbalancing it with the strengths of another" (Jick, 1979: 604). Therefore, quantitative and qualitative methods will be used in the following.

As a first step, Doctrinal Legal Research, which investigates the formulation of R2P as a legal doctrine through the analysis of legal rules, will be undertaken. The purpose of this method is to find out the legal status of a norm (Hart, 1961; Arthurs, 1983). In other words, it will be investigated where and to what extent R2P, developed by the International Commission on Intervention and State Sovereignty (ICISS), has been implemented in International Humanitarian Law (IHL), the UN Charter, the World Summit Outcome Document (WSOD) of 2005 and UNSC Resolutions. The result will be used for the derivation of R2P criteria, which ultimately form a set of options and instruments to be applied by the UN. They are divided into two sub-categories: R2P criteria for the non-use of force and R2P criteria for the potential use of lethal force.

Furthermore, a critical discourse analysis of UNSC Resolutions, presidential statements of the General Assembly (GA) and the UNSC, as well as reports from the Independent International Commission of Inquiry on the Syrian Arab Republic (henceforth it will be referred to as Independent Commission of Inquiry on Syria) will be conducted to find out how UN institutions reacted towards the massive human rights abuse in Syria, and to establish whether their approach to fulfil their responsibility towards the suffering population is decisive. Furthermore it will used to analyse statements by the permanent five UNSC members to find out their interests behind actions or inaction. Critical discourse analyses is especially useful to discover the actors' motives because it "explores how texts construct representations of the world, social relationships and social identities and there is an emphasis on highlighting how such practices and texts are ideologically shaped by relations of power" (Fairclough, 1992 quoted in: Taylor, 2010: 3).

The case study approach has been selected in order to investigate the phenomenon of R2P within its contemporary context. Since there is only a limited number of cases where R2P has been so far applied, given the fact that the concept itself is fairly new, it is necessary to provide a short comparison between Libya and Syria. Firstly, because the civil wars in both countries are similar in their emergence, development, and context, and secondly, because the difference in the UN's reaction to the humanitarian catastrophe in both cases can give insight on how R2P is practiced.

Consequently, empirical data for the case study on Syria will be gathered from several sources, such as the Human Rights Council of the UN (HCR), the Independent Commission of Inquiry on Syria, the European Commission, as well as from non-governmental organisations (NGO's) such as Amnesty International and Human Rights Watch which will be used to gain an understanding on the humanitarian situation in Syria. A cross-referencing of these data will be carried out to increase the validity of the findings. However, the fact that the unstable situation in Syria makes it difficult to get accurate death tolls and circumstances of death will be kept in mind. Consequently, the numbers will be unlikely to be exact, even though the quality of sources will indicate a trend which can be used to draw conclusions on the current situation in Syria.

1.2   Outline of the Dissertation

This dissertation will begin by elaborating the conceptual framework of R2P in Chapter Two, as well as the legal implementation of R2P by the GA in 2005 and the UNSC in 2006. Chapter Two will also lay out the aforementioned criteria for the analysis. Chapter Three will commence with a presentation of the emergence of the Syrian conflict in 2011 and the current situation, before subsequently investigating the measures already taken by the international community. The attention will be on non-military measures, such as mediation and sanctions, and the consensus finding process in the UN. Additionally, R2P criteria will be applied in order to determine whether they are fulfilled in the Syrian case. Chapter Four will go beyond current measures, and will examine whether the Syrian civil war is a case for the use of lethal force authorised by the UNSC. It will thus focus on the scale of violence and human rights abuse in Syria, classified as crimes against humanity and war crimes, and on its implications on regional and global peace and security. In order to do this, the second category of the aforementioned criteria from Chapter Two will be applied. Chapter Five will look at the interests of the five permanent members of the UNSC to find the motives behind their (in)action. Chapter Six will reflect on the implications of a military intervention under R2P in Syria, and will offer an outlook on the future credibility of the UN in case of a failure to end mass atrocities in Syria.

2   Conceptual Framework

2.1   From Sovereignty as Authority to Sovereignty as Responsibility

In order to prevent further humanitarian catastrophes, such as those experienced in the Second World War, the UN was established with the aim "to form an international community based on respect for the dignity of human beings" (Breau, 2005:221). To achieve this goal, members of the UN passed a number of multinational treaties and created laws, among them the Universal Declaration of Human Rights, the Geneva Convention and its Additional Protocols, and IHL in general (Barry and Southwood, 2011), to ensure that individual's human rights would be protected and peace preserved. However, these only oblige states to respect the human rights of their own citizens: conversely they have no obligation towards people outside of their borders (Woodhouse and Ramsbotham, 1998). Consequently, state sovereignty became an important principle in order to protect citizens from external threats, based on the assumption that respect for the sovereignty of other states increases international peace (ibid). However, the possibility that a state might not protect its population, but might instead be the perpetrator, was overlooked. In such cases, humanitarian intervention, defined as "an act of intervention in the internal affairs of another country with the view to ending the physical suffering caused by the disintegration or the gross misuse of the authority of the state, and helping create conditions in which a viable structure of civil authority can emerge" (Parekh, 1997: 55), seems to be an option.

However, during its first forty-five years of existence, the UN stressed that it promotes the non-use of force and non-intervention in a sovereign state's affairs without the sovereign's consent, regardless of the severity of human rights violations (Roberts, 2006). This understanding of the UN's role was challenged in the 1990s due to internal conflicts beginning to outnumber conflicts among states and the humanitarian emergencies in

Somalia, Rwanda and Yugoslavia, during which hundreds of thousands of people were slaughtered and suffered mass atrocities (Weiss and Thakur, 2010:76).

Therefore, the question arises of what the international community, represented by the UN, should do when the shared ideal of a right to life and dignity is violated to an extreme extent. The incidents in the 1990s clearly showed that the instruments of the UN, namely peacekeeping and conflict management, could not provide relief in situations where the state sovereign rejected external help or was itself the abuser. Although there were calls for a legalisation of humanitarian intervention, no consensus was reached on when and how to intervene, and how regional organisations such as the North Atlantic Treaty Organisation (NATO) or individual states should be authorised to enter an internal conflict with potential lethal force in order to protect civilians (Breau, 2005). Ultimately, the UN's credibility as the main human rights organisation was endangered through its inability to enforce its own laws and principles.

On the one hand, most of the UN members states were shocked by the mass atrocities in the 1990s, and the GA as well as the UNSC demonstrated their commitment to human rights in various resolutions (Weiss and Thakur, 2010). On the other hand, a lot of countries, most of them developing countries, worried about any practice that would challenge state sovereignty (Roberts, 2006). According to Jennifer Welsh (2004), the international community faced a dilemma at the end of the 20th century: how should a compromise be found between what is legally right and what is morally right? Consequently, the Canadian government established the ICISS with the objective to provide a doctrine for the right to intervene, responding to the call of Secretary-General Anan (2000) who declared that the protection of human rights must take priority over state sovereignty.

2.1.1 The ICISS Report 2001 and its R2P Criteria

The commissioners of the ICISS intended to develop a set of criteria with which the UN could make quicker and more efficient decisions in times of humanitarian crisis (Welsh, 2004; Weiss, 2004). The subsequent report, published in 2001 (henceforth referred to as R2P2001) was hotly debated since it was based on a new understanding of sovereignty: sovereignty as responsibility (ICISS, 2001: 8). While the traditional, so-called Westphalian, understanding of state sovereignty only included control over a certain territory and the people within it, the ICISS's definition pins state sovereignty on the sovereign's capability and willingness to protect the dignity and basic rights of all the people within the state (ibid.). Additionally, the commissioners did not write a report on the right to intervene, but changed it to a "responsibility to protect" which had three main advantages. Firstly, the ICISS shifted the focus away from the intervener to the affected population which essentially "prioritizes those suffering from starvation or being raped and the duty of international institutions to respond" (Weiss, 2004: 139). Secondly, the ICISS (2001: 13) made clear that the first responsibility lies with the state, and only if the sovereign does not fulfil this responsibility should the international community interfere. Thirdly, according to the ICISS, R2P is not only concerned with military intervention, but stresses the equal importance of the three core principles: the *Responsibility to Prevent*, the *Responsibility to React* and the *Responsibility to Rebuild* (ibid.).

The *Responsibility to Prevent* demands more awareness of the early signs of human rights abuse, and support for a state sovereigns to fulfil their responsibilities towards their citizens with the objective of preventing a conflict from escalating (Bellamy, 2009; ICISS; 2001). The second core principle, the *Responsibility to React,* is the most controversial part of R2P2001 since it includes the use of lethal force. However, the content of the *Responsibility to React* mostly deals with a duty to react to situation where the protection of human lives and dignity from mass atrocities is not guaranteed, and stresses that this includes political, economic and judicial measures (ICISS, 2001). In extreme cases, the last resort is a military intervention, and R2P2001 presents a threshold of six principles which must be fulfilled before a military intervention is justified (Evans and Sahnoun, 2002). These include: *Just Cause*, *Right Intention*, *Proportional Means*, *Right Authority* and *Reasonable Prospects* (ICISS, 2001: 32). R2P2001's last core principle is the *Responsibility to Rebuild*. The ICISS's intention was to make interveners commit to rebuild that which is destroyed during the intervention with the objective that a solid post-conflict reconstruction would create conditions for a long-lasting peace (ibid.).

R2P2001 was deemed revolutionary since it includes original ideas from Just War Theory, further enhancing them by adapting them to the contemporary moral demand for a better protection of human beings from mass atrocities (Evans and Sahnoun, 2002). Nevertheless, even though the ICISS report fuelled the debates about humanitarian intervention, it was still only a report from an independent commission, and was not endorsed by the international community. Therefore, the ICISS and Kofi Annan decided to present the report to the GA during the 2005 World Summit, hoping that it would be implemented quickly (Annan, 2000). In October 2005, the GA of the United Nations unanimously accepted R2P in its World Summit Outcome Document (WSOD). In April 2006, after six months of negotiations, the UNSC affirmed the result of the WSOD in Resolution 1674 (henceforth the R2P version passed by the GA and the UNSC will be referred to as R2P2006). But what do these resolutions mean for R2P?

2.2   Analysis of the Implementation of R2P

The applicability of R2P on cases naturally depends on its legal status. Consequently, it is impossible to understand to what extent the international community committed itself to the ideas of the ICISS without defining whether the implementation of R2P formalised it into a law, a treaty or a norm. Hence, the following section will explore the implementation of R2P2001, and will thus form the basis for the criteria derivation for the case study in a later section.

2.2.1   Legal Implementation of R2P

In order to establish whether R2P principles are binding for international actors, extensive research has been undertaken for the implementation of R2P in UN Resolutions, Conventions, and the UN Charter, the results of which have then been systematically compared to the R2P2001 criteria of the ICISS (see Table 1 in Appendix for details). The main result of the Doctrinal Legal Research is that most R2P principles have indeed been implemented, and that R2P has been treated as a law. The findings of the research are thus twofold: Firstly, R2P2001 is not as revolutionary as first believed, since some of its features were already part of international law before the ICISS Report. For example, the criteria *Last Resort* (UN Charter, Art. 42) and *Proportionality* (ibid; Additional Protocol I) were binding for all Member States before 2005. Secondly, R2P, as it can be practiced today, is not that different from R2P2001 even though it is criticised by R2P advocates, such as Weiss (2007: 117), as "R2P lite". It is true that there are some differences between R2P2001 and R2P2006, among others that R2P2006 only allows a case-by-case evaluation (WSOD, 2005: § 138), and that the *Just Cause* of a military intervention must be a threat to international peace and security, including humanitarian disasters as only one of many potential threats (WSOD, 2005; UN Charter, Article 24; UNSC Res. 1296, 2000). Furthermore, the *Right Authority* for the use of force implemented in UN documents is only the UNSC (WSOD, 2005: § 139; UN Charter Chapter VII). Therefore, the ICISS's (2001) proposition to allow the GA to legitimately intervene in cases where the UNSC fails to react to mass atrocities in a timely and decisive manner has not been implemented. Moreover, the criteria *Reasonable Prospects* and *Right Intention* cannot be found in any legal or political document.

However, the UN passed a *Responsibility to Prevent* by agreeing to "assist[ing] those which are under stress before crises and conflicts break out" (WSOD, 2005: § 138, 139). Additionally, the UN accepted its *Responsibility to React* to mass atrocities and only restricted it to genocide, war crimes, ethnic cleansing and crimes against humanity (WSOD, 2005: §138, 139), which is also partly incorporated into the Genocide Convention (1948: §8). Therefore, the UN gave R2P more focus instead of adopting the very general proposition of the ICISS (2011: 12) to act in cases of "large scale loss of life (actual or apprehended) and [...] large ethnic cleansing". Likewise, the UN agreed to use "appropriate diplomatic, humanitarian and other peaceful means [...] to help protect populations from genocide, war crimes, ethnic cleansing and crimes against humanity" (WSOD, 2005: §139). Moreover, the UN passed the *Responsibility to Rebuild* by setting up the Peacebuilding Commission in order to "[...] assist[ing] parties of conflicts to end hostilities and emerge towards recovery, reconstruction and development and in mobilizing sustained international attention and assistance" (UNSC Res. 1645, 2005: 1).

Nevertheless, the parts of R2P2001 which were adopted verbatim by the international community were agreed upon in the WSOD and UNSC Resolutions which makes them legally recommendatory for future decisions, despite not being legally binding (Stahn, 2007). However, R2P advocates have to acknowledge that even though one cannot argue that R2P is a law, the evidence presented above demonstrates the fact that it mirrors international law.

Moreover, the comparison shows that most of R2P2001 principles have indeed been implemented. This is supported by the fact that UNSC has referred to R2P2006 in twenty-three of its resolutions since 2005, justifying its decisions to act in a certain way, mostly to sanction, to send peacekeeping troops or to condemn mass atrocities, as a result of a state's negligence to protect its citizens (see Table 2 in Appendix). In UNSC Resolution 1973 (2011) it even authorised the use of force against the Gaddafi regime in Libya. Additionally, the UN has continued to incorporate R2P in UN practice, for example by founding the Mediation Support Unit and creating the position of the Special Representative on the Prevention of Genocide and Mass Atrocities (Breakey, 2012).

This leads to the conclusion that, even though R2P2006 cannot be called state practice yet, it is part of *Jug Cogens* which is "a body of principles recognized by the international community as being fundamental to the maintenance of international order [...] from which no derogation is permitted" (West's Encyclopedia of American Law, 2008). These principles, agreed upon by the UN, concern threats to international peace and security, the use of force and humanitarian elements, such as genocide, slavery and nowadays also considerable abuse of human rights. In other words, R2P might not be a law, but it is a legal norm to which the UN has committed itself. Hence, the UN can be held to maintain its pledge to prevent and react to mass atrocities, and to rebuild post conflict. Its failure to do so will thus harm the foundation and credibility of the UN. Based on this conclusion, a set of criteria can be derived.

2.3   Deriving Criteria for the Case Study

For the case study on Syria, the criteria, derived from R2P in its legal implementation recently discussed, are divided into two main categories: the first deals with the *Responsibility to Prevent* measures undertaken, while the second includes the *Responsibility to React* criteria. The latter is subdivided into peaceful instruments, and the potential use of force. As a result, the following research design emerges and will be applied to Syria:

1. Responsibility to Prevent: Measures undertaken to prevent a humanitarian emergency from escalating

2. Responsibility to React:

   a. Peaceful instruments: The use of "appropriate diplomatic, humanitarian and other peaceful means […] to help protect […]" (WSOD, 2005: § 139) the Syrian population

   b. Potential military Intervention: Is Syria a case for the permissible and legal authorisation of force by the UN? The following criteria must be fulfilled:

      i. *Just Cause:* One of the following is applicable in the case

         - Genocide

         - War crimes

         - Crimes against humanity

         - Ethnic cleansing

      ii. *Last Resort:* All peaceful means have been exhausted and have no or little prospect of being successful

      iii. Occurrence of a *Threat to International Peace and security*

Since the Syrian conflict is still ongoing, the *Responsibility to Rebuild* will not be discussed here. Furthermore, *Proportionality* and *Right Authority* are also excluded, the first because it is an operating principle which is applicable when the decision has already been made to conduct a military intervention, and the measures to be undertaken are being discussed. The second is excluded because a discussion on who can authorise the use of force is so complex, especially in its legal implications, that it is beyond the scope of this study. Hence, in accordance with the UN Charter, the UNSC will be understood as the sole authority to legitimise the use of force.

2.3.1 The Libyan Case: the First Military Intervention under R2P

Turning now to the extent to which R2P has been practiced, this section will shortly give a brief overview of the Libyan civil war in 2011. This was the first case in which the UN prioritised the human rights of a population over the rights of the government to sovereignty.

In February 2011, anti-government protests began in Libya following the Arab spring uprisings (Anderson, 2011). When the protest spread across Libya, Gaddafi's government used excessive force against the protestors: according to Human Rights Watch (2012), live fire was used, hundreds of Libyans allegedly involved in the anti-government demonstrations were arrested, and protestors were executed. Furthermore, published reports bore witness to the sexual assault of men and women, the use of torture, and child soldiers by Gaddafi forces (Independent Commission of Inquiry on Libya, 2011; Human Rights Watch, 2012). This resulted in at least 170,000 Libyans fleeing to neighbouring countries within the first ten days in order to escape the violence (UNHCR, 2011: 3), countries which were themselves dealing with the turmoil of regime changes (Kuperman,

2013). Within two weeks, the Libyan conflict had developed to a full civil war (Williams, 2011).

If the R2P criteria from the last section are applied to the Libyan case it becomes obvious that the UN reacted quickly and attempted to fulfil its responsibility to protect. The UN firstly followed its *Responsibility to Prevent* by acknowledging the early signs of warnings and establishing an independent commission to investigate the allegations reported by NGOs, and furthermore started to negotiate with the Gaddafi regime to cease the violence against civilians (A/HRC/14/44, 2011). Additionally, the UNSC passed Resolution 1970 in February 2011 condemning the gross and systematic human rights violations in the country, especially the indiscriminate attacks against peaceful protestors, classifying these as crimes against humanity. When it became clear within days that the security situation in Libya had deteriorated and developed into a civil war, the UN then fulfilled its *Responsibility to React* by setting various coercive measures in place, such as financial sanctions and arms embargos, and furthermore referred the situation in Libya to the Prosecutor of the International Criminal Court (ICC) (Doyle, 2011; Anderson, 2011). However, Gaddafi continued to use force against the Libyan population, denied his population access to humanitarian aid, and showed no interest in engaging in a dialogue with the opposition (Kuperman, 2013).

Accordingly, the international community concluded that further diplomatic attempts to solve the situation in Libya were unlikely to succeed and declared all peaceful instruments of the *Responsibility to React* as exhausted (Doyle, 2011). As a result, the UNSC passed Resolution 1973 in March, determining that that the situation in Libya constituted a threat to international peace and security and authorising military action under Chapter VII of the Charter. It thus paved the way for NATO to conduct a no-fly zone[1] (Thakur, 2011).

Since the UNSC needed only one month to conclude that military force constituted Last Resort, it could be argued that not all the peaceful options available had been tried before legitimising the use of force (ibid). Nevertheless, the UNSC declared that further non-military action would only contribute to deteriorating the conflict (UNSC Res. 1973, 2011). Additionally, the UNSC received support from the Gulf Cooperation Council (GCC) which asked the UNSC to "take all necessary measures to protect civilians, including enforcing a no-fly zone over Libya" (GCC, 2011, in: Lauterpacht Centre, 2011). Furthermore, the *Just Cause* criteria was fulfilled: there was evidence of crimes against humanity and war crimes, and these were seen as severe enough to be a threat to international peace and security (ibid; Vanderwalle, 2011).

Consequently, Resolution 1973 marked a milestone for R2P since, for the first time, the UNSC authorised Members States to go to war against a regime in order to protect civilians. Six months later, the civil war was declared to be over and R2P was celebrated as a success. Bellamy (2011:198) states that the Libyan case indicated that "governments can no longer subject their populations to massive abuse without attracting international criticism, engagement and possible coercion". However, the intervention has also been severely criticised, particularly by Russia and China, who abstained from the vote on Resolution 1973, for 'mission creep' (Thakur, 2011). They argue that the 'coalition of the willing', which conducted the no-fly zone, did take it too far by becoming politically involved and aiding the opposition to change regime (ibid).

---

[1] The author is aware of the fact that the relationship between the UN and NATO has been the matter of much debate, especially in the context of the Libya intervention. However, this complex discussion will not be included here since it will not contribute to the aim of this study. See Kaplan (2013), Deen-Racsmány (2000), Hough (2004) for more information.

In summary, this analysis presents enough evidence to support the argument made in section 2.3.: R2P is indeed a Jus Cogens, a legal norm, since it was seen in the Libyan case as sufficient to justify the breach of the oldest principle of international society, the right to territorial integrity, in order to fulfil another principle, the protection of civilians. The criteria derived in the last section, *Responsibility to Prevent, Responsibility to React,* and additionally the criteria for a military intervention, *Just Cause, Last Resort* and *Threat to International Peace and Security,* were met, and a military intervention was thus justified. Therefore, it is at this point of no importance whether the intervention conducted by NATO was in accordance with Resolution 1973. Instead, the main result is that the Libyan case demonstrates that the use of force to protect civilians in other countries was now no longer only a theoretical possibility (Williams, 2011).

3   Syria Part I: Peaceful Instruments of R2P in Practice

The Chapter now turns to the Syrian civil war and will investigate whether the UN fulfilled its *Responsibility to Prevent* the conflict from escalating and whether it has reacted to the mass atrocities according to its *Responsibility to React*. Has the UN done everything in its power to protect the Syrian population?

3.1   The Emergence of the Syrian Conflict

Since 1970, the al-Assad family and the socialist Ba'ath Party have been ruling Syria. Ever since, political and religious tensions have been part of Syrian political life, mostly due to the rival ideologies of the regime's ruling Alawite minority (16% of the population), which follows the Baathist socialism, and the Sunni Muslim majority (76%), which adheres to Islamic law (Jaddaliyya, 2014). The Ba'ath regime upholds a strictly authoritarian rule, and successfully oppressed any form of opposition for more than three decades (Khashan, 2011).

In 2000, Bashar al-Assad took over as President and started reforms promising more political freedom. However, the reforms were mainly of economic character, diverging from the socialist orientation of his father towards capitalism (Hinnebusch, 2012). The majority of the population did not benefit politically or economically. Instead, power and wealth remained exclusive to the Alawite minority (Haddad, 2012). The Arab Spring in 2011 served as a trigger and, like in Libya, the "demonstration effect" spilled over to Syria, fostered by the increased access to the internet, social media and other communication tools (Khashan, 2013). Therefore, exiled Syrians in particular played a crucial role at the beginning of the Syrian uprising since they used the internet to encourage rebellion (Hinnebusch, 2012).

In March 2011, protests began in the tribal and predominately Sunni rural town Daraa, but shortly afterwards disparate acts occurred in other, predominately non-Alawite, towns with demands for more political and economic freedom, and calls for an amnesty for all political prisoners (Heydemann, 2013). When the regime reacted to the peaceful protests with violence, closed the border, and furthermore restricted the media's influence, the calls for reforms quickly became calls for a regime change and spread to larger cities, such as Homs (Ryan, 2012; Ismail, 2013). Bashar al-Assad called the uprising a result of foreign conspiracy and denied the scale of violence conducted by government troops (International Crisis Group, 2011). However, Human Rights Watch (2012) reported that government forces killed at least 3,500 protestors in the first few months and arbitrarily detained thousands, a large number of them children under the age of eighteen. Afterwards, the Syrian government implemented a number of reforms in an unsuccessful attempt to subdue the protest movement by lifting the state of emergency and issuing two general amnesties which benefited a small group of political prisoners (ibid.).

Nevertheless, the protestors were not satisfied and began to loosely organise themselves in several split organisations, among others the Syrian National Council, which mostly consists of exiled Syrians; and the Free Syrian Army (FSA), which consists of former soldiers of the Syrian military and armed rebels; the Muslim Brotherhood, which has historically been the focus of the regime's oppression; and then several military groups with foreign jihad fighters (ICRtoP, 2014; Landis, 2012). The Syrian National Council tried to unify the opposition movements and proclaimed a hierarchy among them with the Syrian National Council as the representative of the Syrian people (Landis, 2012). Yet this was mostly fictional since the several groups have been working independently, and have even been pursuing different, and often contradictory, political goals (Van Dam, 2011).

But why have the several opposition groups been unable to unite as the Libyans did? The reason for this is, firstly, that the groups are not only divided into Islamists and secular Syrians but that there is "rather a divide between those living abroad and those fighting on the inside, who are waging the daily battles on the street" (Landis, 2012: 77). Secondly, this results in different political goals: the Syrian National Council's objective, for example, is to transform Syria into a modern democratic state (Hanano, 2012) whilst the Muslim Brotherhood thrives for an Islamic state (Hussein, 2013). Therefore, the Syrian National Council, which had the most potential to become a leading opposition group, has failed to integrate Syrian militia and rebels.

In August 2011, the FSA began to attack government forces in an attempt to gain control over Homs. This marked the beginning of the armed conflict between the opposition groups and the regime, which quickly evolved into a full civil war with several armed opposition groups and government security forces subjecting civilians to massive human rights abuse (Independent Commission of Inquiry on Syria, 2011). This continued throughout the period covered in this dissertation, namely March 2011 to June 2014.

3.2 Measures Undertaken by the International Community so far: Application of R2P Criteria

3.2.1 Responsibility to Prevent

As described above, the peaceful protests quickly evolved into an armed conflict. Thus, the question arises whether the international community attempted to prevent the conflict's escalation.

Firstly, one has to look whether there were early signs that the conflict might evolve into a civil war. The al-Assad family had participated in massacres against the opposition in the past, for example in the Hama massacre perpetrated by Bashar al-Assad's father in 1982 (Ismail, 2011), which indicated the extent to which the regime would go to preserve its power. Since then, rights groups, such as Genocide Watch (2012), reported that the Ba'ath regime have been systematically abusing human rights through arbitrary detention, torture and execution. The deliberate targeting of civilians at the beginning of the peaceful protests, especially the targeting of particular groups, mostly Sunni Muslims, further demonstrated that Assad does not comply with international law and the Human Rights Charter (Landis, 2012). Moreover, the Syrian government has denied its participation in the use of force against civilians, and instead accused Islamist terrorists of fuelling the conflict (Heydemann, 2013). In addition, from March 2011 onwards the regime has been refusing humanitarian access to its population which has quickly resulted in shortages of food, water and basic healthcare supplies (A/HRC/14/44, 2011).

In short, the Syrian government became known for its disregard for human rights and international law, and its actions during the Arab Spring demonstrated its unwillingness to engage in dialogue with the opposition. Instead, Bashar al-Assad used excessive force against his people. This reaction, and the quick radicalisation of the opposition groups, resulted in the armed conflict which started in summer 2011. The international community thus had around three months to react to the deteriorating situation in Syria, and to prevent an escalation according to R2P, more than triple the time they needed in the Libyan case to exhaust all peaceful measures.

However, the situation today clearly demonstrates the international community's failure to fulfil its *Responsibility to Prevent*. The UNHCR reacted first by condemning "the use of lethal violence against peaceful protestors" (A/HCR/Res/s-16/2, 2011: 3) in April. In August, it then established the Independent Commission of Inquiry on Syria to investigate the alleged human rights violations (A/HCR/Res/s-17/1, 2011). Nevertheless, apart from these two resolutions, there was no reaction whatsoever from the UN, including no UNSC statement or resolution regarding the situation in Syria, in the months leading up to the armed conflict. Therefore, it is debatable whether the UN even attempted to prevent the situation in Syria from escalating since it remained silent during a period in which the opposition group had not yet taken up arms, and it thus might have been more likely to foster a dialogue between the opposition and the government.

Although establishing an investigative commission was necessary, its first report, published in November 2011, was nevertheless too late to present any information enabling decisions to act to be made. By August opposition groups and government security forces were fighting for control over Syrian territory: yet the UN failed to act despite the early warning signs, and regardless of the media and NGO reports on the human rights violations committed by all parties at that time. Consequently, the international community failed to fulfil its responsibility to prevent.

3.2.2 Responsibility to React

When the Independent Commission of Inquiry on Syria (2011) published its first report, it presented evidence that gross human rights violations had been occurring in Syria, mostly committed by government forces. Additionally, it stated that these violations constituted crimes against humanity and called upon State Members and the Human Rights Council to bring the violators to justice, and furthermore, to refer the situation in Syria to the ICC (ibid.). The UN Commissioner for Human Rights, Navi Pillay, reported in December 2011 that more than 5,000 had died and that thousands were being detained, tortured or executed (UN News Centre, 2011). Consequently, the death toll in Syria had more than doubled since August. These facts indicate that the Responsibility to React was applicable.

However, the UN took a further three months to react. In February 2012, it finally appointed Kofi Annan as chief of the Joint Special Envoy of the UN and the Arab League on Syria with the objective of ending the violence, but by remaining neutral rather than promoting regime change (Thomas, 2013). The UN thus followed R2P by attempting to support the existing government to fulfil its responsibility towards its citizens and to function as a mediator between the conflict parties. Annan subsequently presented the Six Point Peace Plan which primarily promoted a political discourse led by the Syrian government to address the population's suffering, a UN observed ceasefire, access to humanitarian aid, and respect for human rights (Hamilton, 2012). The Peace Plan was then presented to Bashar al Assad who endorsed it in March 2012.

On the 14th of April in 2012, the UNSC finally reacted by adopting Resolution 2042 in which it reaffirmed its strong commitment to Syria's sovereignty, authorised a team of 30 unarmed military observers to investigate the violence in Syria and to monitor the implementation of the Peace Plan, and called for an end to the violence. Two weeks later, Resolution 2043 followed which principally condemned the human rights violations committed by the Syrian government and armed opposition groups, and established a UN Supervision Mission in Syria (UNSMIS) for 90 days. This mission, however, was suspended in June 2012 because of the deteriorating security situation and the unwillingness of the parties to seek a peaceful transition (UNSMIS, 2012). Moreover, Kofi Annan tried to engage in a dialogue with the Syrian government which ultimately failed since the Syrian government continued to use excessive force against opposition groups, ultimately resulting in Annan's resignation (Thomas, 2013).

Algerian diplomat and experienced UN politician Lakhar Brahimi followed in his footsteps in September 2012; nevertheless, he, too, was unable to implement a ceasefire (Deutsche Welle, 2012). Brahimi thus resigned in 2014, stating that he faces impossible odds "with a Syrian nation, Middle Easters region and wider international community that have been hopelessly divided in their approaches to ending the conflict." (UN News Centre, 2014). The

Peace Conference in Geneva in 2013 and 2014, at which the National Coalition for Syrian Revolutionary and Opposition Forces and representatives of the Assad government met, failed because none of the participating parties were able to make concessions concerning their demands (ibid.). While the Assad regime claims to be the sole representative of the Syrian people and demands that all opposition forces surrender, the National Coalition of the Opposition Forces, which does not even represent all opposition groups, urges the Assad government to resign and open the way for democratic elections (Sharpiro and Charap, 2014). It is difficult to see any common ground between these contradicting demands.

Consequently, regional organisations and individual states passed their own sanctions trying to force the Syrian government to follow the peace plan and cease the violence. The Arab League reacted first and suspended Syria from their league, before sending observers to Syria to investigate the alleged human rights violations (MacFarquhar, 2011). However, these had to be called back because of the dangerous security situation (Ryan, 2012). Furthermore, the League has been encouraging the UNSC to impose sanctions on Syria and supported the Joint Special Envoy in its attempt to mediate between the conflicting parties (ICRtoP, 2014).

The European Union (EU) members have been able to enforce sanctions which were implemented in February 2012, including travel bans on Syrian government officials, an arms embargo, trade sanctions, and the freezing of Syrian government assets (UK Government, 2013). This was a huge setback for the Assad regime since the EU was Syria's main trading partner, accounting for over 40% of its total trade (Ehtheshami, 2009: 74). The US endorsed similar sanctions and tried to push for joint sanctions in the UNSC (US Treasury Department, 2012).

In contrast, China, Russia and Iran have been continuing to support the Assad regime diplomatically, financially and militarily (Human Rights Watch, 2014) even though Russia has been unilaterally and unsuccessfully trying to convince the Assad regime to make some compromises (Allison, 2013).

The chemical weapon attack in August 2013 might have been expected to change the way the international community reacted towards the mass atrocities in Syria, since the use of chemical weapons is a serious breach of international law; for example that joint actions would either enforce stricter sanctions or even authorise the use of force. The UNSC indeed reacted quickly to reports of attacks by passing a resolution recognizing evidence of the use of chemical weapons in Syria as valid, condemning the attack, and expressing "a strong conviction that those individuals responsible for the use of chemical weapons [...] must be held accountable" (UNSC Res. 2118, 2013: 4). However, there is no discussion on the accountability dimension in the resolution.

Nevertheless, this resolution was exceptional due to the declaration that the further use of these kind of weapons was considered a threat to international peace and security which ultimately justifies the international community to intervene and use lethal force (UNSC Res. 2118, 2013). This assertion was underlined by the fact that, in the event of non-compliance with the UNSC's demand to destroy all chemical weapons immediately under international supervision, the UNSC "would impose Chapter VII measures" (ibid: 4).

The language of the UNSC changed after the chemical attacks. While the aforementioned UNSC Resolutions on Syria in 2012 predominately used the expressions "calls", "condemns" and "asks" (UNSC Res. 2042, 2043, 2059), Resolution 2118 employs "demands" and "decides". This change in vocabulary implied a development within the UNSC: previously a divided, insecure council, it became a strong political body that would not ask but demand compliance with its resolutions. It therefore raised hopes that the UNSC would find a consensus and would be more successful in protecting the Syrian population.

Nonetheless, even though Resolution 2139 in February 2014 (p.2ff)

> "demands that all parties allow delivery of humanitarian assistance, cease depriving civilians of food and medicine indispensable for their survival [...], demands that all parties respect the principle of medical neutrality [...] Strongly condemns the widespread violations of human rights and international humanitarian law by the Syrian authorities, as well as the human rights abuses and violations of international humanitarian law by armed groups...[and] stresses that some of these violations may amount to war crimes and crimes against humanity",

the UNSC does not mention any consequences for non-compliance or any action on its own part. Furthermore, despite the fact that it reminds all conflict parties of their responsibility to discriminate between civilians and combatants, there is no sentence in the resolution declaring the international community's R2P. In contrast, Resolution 2150, which was introduced in 2014, reaffirms R2P, calling on Member States to fight against war crimes, crimes against humanity and genocide, even though it mentions Syria only in the preamble as one of the current humanitarian crises.

However, has the UN used all "diplomatic, humanitarian and other peaceful means [...] to help protect [...]" (WSOD, 2005: § 139) the Syrian population according to its responsibility to react? Even though there have been diplomatic attempts through Annan's and Brahimi's mediation unit, the UN has not been able to agree on sanctions or embargos which could ultimately isolate Syria. Four attempts to find a consensus on such measures in the UNSC failed because of vetoes from Russia and China: the first one in October 2011 (UNSC 10403), the second in February 2012 (UNSC 10536), the third in July 2012 (UNSC 10714) and the last in May 2014 (UNSC Meeting 7180). Whilst the first three intended to threaten the Syrian government with sanctions if it did not stop the violence, the French draft in 2014, supported by more than 60 UN members, called for an investigation by the ICC into the war crimes based on evidence collected by the Independent Commission of Inquiry on Syria. In short, the UN has failed to exhaust all available diplomatic measures because it was not able to find a consensus in its main decision making body, the UNSC.

Furthermore, the diplomatic actions, agreed by the UN, were late and ultimately failed. The UN needed months to establish a mediation unit under Annan and to condemn the human rights violations in Syria. Moreover, during the first twelve months of the conflict, during which thousands of civilians were killed, detained, tortured and displaced, the UNSC was only able to send unarmed observers to Syria. Annan's and Brahimi's attempts to act as mediators between the warring parties were unsuccessful because of three main reasons: firstly, the Envoy was created too late because of the UNSC's deadlock, which meant that the conflict had already escalated such that the conflicting parties had become so obstinate in their positions that neither side were prepared to make concessions. As a result, the probability of a ceasefire was low even from the outset of the Special Envoy's work (Thomas, 2013). Secondly, the Joint Special Envoy did not have a united international community behind it which might advocate the efforts of mediation by adopting sanctions and embargos (ibid.). The sanctions imposed by individual states and regional organisations did not help to isolate the Syrian government and thus force it to engage in negotiations since Syria still had support from main global actors, namely Russia and China. Thirdly, the extent to which the violence had escalated was greater than the observer mission was equipped for. According to Doyle (2012), the 300 men strong mission was "slow to deploy and too small".

Since the human suffering in Syria reached such dramatic scale, UN agencies and NGOs, financially supported by the US, the EU and the Arab League, have been trying to bring some relief to the Syrians. However, it has been virtually impossible, especially in opposition-controlled areas, to deliver essential medical supplies and food to those in need (European Commission, 2014). Additionally, humanitarian agencies have also suffered losses: since 2011, around 50 humanitarian workers have been killed, UN and Red Cross' vehicles have been subjected to attacks, and UN personnel has been kidnapped and held to ransom by opposition groups (ibid). It seems that the security and safety of humanitarian workers cannot be guaranteed since IHL, which ought to protect civilians and medical personnel, is not respected in Syria (Abrams, 2014). As a result, humanitarian agencies have called back most of their personnel and, instead, are now concentrating on Syrian refugees in the neighbour countries. Consequently, the scale of suffering in Syria is increasing (European Commission, 2014). The civil war has been worsening steadily and, since September 2013, the rebels have even been fighting each other, too, starting with an attack by the terrorist organisation Islamic State of Iraq and Syria (ISIS)[2] on the FSA (ICRtoP, 2014).

In conclusion, the UN could, and should, have cooperated better, especially in the UNSC, with regard to sanctions and embargos, in order to exhaust all available diplomatic means. Even though unilateral action attempted to compensate for the UN's failure to adopt joint measures, the support from China and Russia prevented Assad's regime from being pressured into making any concessions. Therefore, the UN failed to fulfil its responsibility to protect.

---

[2] Also known as the Islamic State of Iraq and the Levant (Whitnall, 2014)

4   Syria Part II: Military Intervention in Syria

At this point, after three years of ongoing war, it seems that the violence in Syria has escalated beyond the point where further diplomatic attempts could solve the conflict. All warring parties have failed to show an interest in ending the civil war by not following the UN's Six Point Peace Plan, nor making any concessions during meetings, such as the two Geneva conferences, and instead increasing the scale of violence. Thus, the following question arises: does the Syrian case fulfil all of the conditions for a military intervention and, as such, justify the use of force against the Syrian regime?

4.1   Just Cause

Firstly, it must be determined whether there violence in Syria has reached the scale that is regarded by R2P as a *Just Cause* for a military intervention. As explained in Chapter 2, the international community defined *Just Cause* as the existence of evidence for genocide, war crimes, crimes against humanity and ethnic cleansing (WSOD, 2005). It is clear that in Syria two of these are present and have been committed by all warring parties, namely war crimes and crimes against humanity.

The most important aspect of IHL is the discrimination between those who directly participate in the war and civilians, amongst which the protection of women and children has a special status (Additional Protocol I, Art. 48). However, UN Secretary General Ban-Ki Moon (2014, in: UN Secretary Report to the UNSC on Children and Armed Conflict in Syria, 2014: 4) reported that FSA- affiliated and other armed opposition groups have conducted air strikes and shelling on densely populated areas, which has killed civilians and damaged infrastructure, especially health and education facilities. Additionally, several armed opposition groups have recruited and used children in their fight against the Assad regime. Moreover, government and opposition forces are using schools as "military barracks, operational bases, sniper posting or detention facilities, including while children [are] attending classes, putting them at extreme risk of being attacked" (ibd: 19).

Furthermore, Human Rights Watch (2014) reported that since July, and even more since October 2013, the Syrian government has been using cluster bombs, which are banned by the international community and defined as a breach of IHL. On top of that, the regime used chemical weapons in August 2013 against civilians, including children "on a relatively large scale" (UN Mission to Investigate Allegations of the Use of Chemical Weapons in the Syrian Arab Republic, 2013: 2) which, according to Human Rights Watch (2013: 14), resulted in between 80 and 103 deaths and over 3,600 injured individuals.

Government forces have been besieging large areas of the country where they only randomly allow food and medical supplies' deliveries. So far, in the besieged Yamouk district at the border of Damascus alone, 128 people have reportedly starved to death, 60% are reported to be suffering from malnutrition while the number of people dying because of a lack of access to basic medicine can only be estimated (Amnesty International, 2014b). Actions such as collective starving or depriving civilians of objects which are indispensable to their survival are defined as war crimes (ICRC Customary Law Study, Rule 156).

Additionally, crimes against humanity are occurring in Syria, for example the use of sexual violence as a weapon of warfare against all ages, including children, especially against boys (UN Secretary General Report, 2014). Ban-Ki Moon also presented evidence of crimes against humanity in state controlled facilities where individuals were victims of beatings with metal clubs and whips, electric shocks including to the genitals, sexual violence, mock executions, cigarette burns, sleep deprivation, and exposure to the torture of relatives (ibid: 6). The report also indicates that the UN has received allegations that armed opposition groups have treated alleged government supporters similarly (ibid.).

Moreover, there is strong evidence that Assad's soldiers have committed mass murder. One incident occurred, for example, in Homs in May 2012 when 100 individuals, 45 of which were children under the age of fifteen, were shot at close range and afterwards buried in mass graves (ibid.).

As a result, so far more than 160,000 Syrians have died in the Syrian civil war while the numbers of civilians suffering in besieged areas, detention facilities, or whilst fleeing to neighbouring countries is estimated to amount to millions (ibid.; European Commission, 2014a: 1).

In summary, there is strong evidence that war crimes and crimes against humanity have been conducted in the Syrian civil war which makes the suffering of the population extreme. Therefore, the *Just Cause* condition for military action under R2P is fulfilled.

4.2   Last Resort

When the use of force is considered, according to the R2P criteria, it is necessary to investigate whether all the peaceful instruments intended to solve the conflict have been unsuccessful so far and are unlikely to be adequate in the future. Military action must be the only option left to try, or, in other words, it must be of *Last Resort*.

At present there are no set rules which determine when the last resort has been reached. Nevertheless, there are certain facts which indicate an internal solution to the conflict is remote, or even non-existent. Firstly, the aforementioned evidence for mass atrocities committed by all conflict parties ultimately means that no civilian in Syria is safe, regardless of their affiliation. Secondly, a ceasefire has not occurred despite the efforts of the international community. The mediation and peace plans conducted by the UN diplomats Annan, and Brahimi, and the sanctions passed by individual countries and regional organisations have failed to establish peace within Syria. Instead, the humanitarian situation has deteriorated over the last three years and the conflict is increasingly affecting other Middle Eastern states.

Thomas (2013: 29) thus argues that "it is relatively clear that the conflict has escalated past the point at which sanctions could have any tangible effects on the behaviour of the regime and bring about a peaceful resolution". Indeed, statistics from other armed conflicts prove that the more a conflict progresses, the more all conflict parties become desperate and are less likely to find a peaceful solution (Snidal, 2006). Hence, sanctions and embargos are only a successful instrument of international relations if the targeted states and officials react rationally to the limitations imposed upon them. With regards to Syria however "the likeliness of a positive outcome for sanctions has been significantly reduced now that the regime's survival is at stake" (Thomas, 2013: 34).

Furthermore, Brahimi (2013) stated that "the longer the conflict continues, the more diffi-cult it will be to repair the physical damage and heal the deep physical and psychological wounds inflicted on the people". Even though at this point Brahimi still urged for a diplomatic solution, his resignation one year later indicated that the battle lines within Syria are too firmly set to encourage a surrender from either of the conflict partied. The international community's further hesitation to use force might thus only make rebuilding Syria post-conflict it more difficult, costly and time-consuming.

So, what does it mean if all peaceful instruments tried so far have failed, and those not yet tried are likely to fail? The conclusion is that the Syrian conflict is at a point where a military intervention from the international community has indeed become a *Last Resort*.

4.3   A Threat to International Peace and Security
The most important condition for the UNSC's authorisation of force on behalf of a suffering population against the will of the people's sovereign is, according to the aforementioned

R2P criteria from chapter 2, that the internal conflict must pose a threat to international peace and security.

With regard to Syria, the involvement of radical Islamist groups, among them the Al-Qaeda splinter group Islamic State of Iraq and Syria (ISIS), whose practice of mass executions, torture and sexual violence is proven by UN agencies, is a dangerous development of the conflict (Nebehay, 2014). The groups fighting in Syria for the establishment of an Islamic state have benefitted from the conflict the most, since ISIS has been able to recruit Syrian and foreign jihad soldiers to fight for their cause. The increased foreign jihad presence in Syria is fuelling the armed conflict since it provides radical opposition groups with soldiers and new weapons. This, for example, helped ISIS to gain control over large areas of Syria, including two lucrative oil fields (Al-Akhabar, 2014; Abrams, 2014). The US government estimates that around 12,000 fighters with various ethnic and cultural backgrounds have so far joined the fight in Syria, among them not only ISIS' Sunni fighters, but also Shia Forces, namely Iranian and Hezbollah (Abrams, 2014). As a result of their increased jihadi forces, ISIS was able to assemble in Syria and cross the Syrian border to Iraq in order to edge the Americans and the current Iraqi government out (Chulov, 2013). Subsequently, ISIS played a considerable role in throwing Iraq back into turmoil, escalating in 2014, with northern Iraq currently under ISIS control and suffering "heavy human casualties including children, the displacement of more than one million Iraqi civilians, and threats against all religious and ethnic groups" (UNSC Res. 2169, 2014: 1).

As a result of the deteriorating security situation in Syria, 2.9 million Syrians have left the country and are living in refugee camps in Egypt and Turkey, but mostly in Lebanon, Iraq, and Jordan, the last three countries already hosting millions of Palestinian refugees (UNHCR, 2014). Apart from the Syrian refugees' poor living conditions, the host countries' current and long-term economic and social development, itself already fragile before the outbreak of the Syrian civil war, are under pressure. Lebanon, for example, a country with a total population of six million, hosts around 1,093,069 refugees (World Food Programme, 2014: 6; European Commission, 2014a). Consequently, the elevated crime rate and a shortage of basic food and health supplies has put pressure on the local economy (European Commission, 2014a). Moreover, foreign direct investment and tourism has declined, especially in Lebanon, due to the civil war in its neighbouring country (Trading Economics, 2014). Also, the rising competition on the labour market has lowered wages for the few who find work, which has led to lower gross domestic product growth rates (ibid). Hence, the struggle with the refugee influx has reduced the host countries' chances for sustainable development and could result in a deeper regional economic crisis. The European Commission (2014a) also reports rising tensions between refugees and the local population which make it difficult for the host states' government to maintain their internal peace.

In summary, it can indeed be argued that the Syrian conflict is a threat to international peace and security since there is strong evidence that the civil war in Syria is endangering the already unstable security situation in the Middle East. Firstly, through the steady refugee flow which is destabilising Syria's neighbours' social peace and economy, and secondly through the provision of a safe haven for extremist groups who use the chaos in Syria to pursue their radical goals in the Middle East. Of course, the deterioration of the security situation in the Middle East in the last few years was not caused by the Syrian conflict alone. However, it definitely contributed to the armed rebellion in Iraq. Ultimately, the Middle Eastern states' inability to control Islamist extremists in the region threatens not only regional but also international security.

Moreover, the Middle Eastern states' capacities to carry out their responsibilities towards the Syrian refugees and their own population is continuously decreasing. This alone could justify a military intervention in Syria since the international community already has to assist the Lebanese and Jordan sovereigns to fulfil their R2P and will have to invest more, financially, personnel-wise and time-wise, if the humanitarian and security situation continues to worsen. Therefore, a failure to act according to the military principles of R2P in Syria will only lead to further cases of humanitarian disasters and force the international community to intervene in order to prevent the whole region from collapsing.

Consequently, the international community, which has so far failed to prevent the escalation of the Syrian conflict and to act upon its commitment to protect the population against mass atrocities, could legally and morally authorise force. Moreover, had the UN intervened militarily in Syria, they might have avoided the current terror in Iraq by Islamist extremists and the slow economic, social and political destabilisation in Syria's other neighbouring countries. However, as explained in chapter three, the UNSC has even had difficulties to find a consensus on the peaceful instruments of R2P. Thus, it is highly unlikely that the permanent five will pass a resolution authorising a military intervention as it did in the Libyan case.

5 Global Actors: Idealism vs. Practice

The previous chapters have raised various important issues concerning R2P in the case of Syria, but one key question has come to light as a result of analysing the situation more closely: why does the UNSC not seem to be able to reach a consensus on how to act according to their responsibility to protect the Syrian population?

China and Russia have so far been using their veto power to prevent sanctions or a military intervention from being implemented in Syria. Russia has even been supporting Assad diplomatically in the UNSC and militarily by supplying the regime with arms whilst China has kept a relative low profile (Allison, 2013). Russia's position can be attributed to two main factors: firstly, Russia's narrative constantly argues "against external interference" (UNSC Res. 2042, 2012; Res. 2059, 2012; Res. 2043, 2012) of any kind. In the Concept of Foreign Policy of the Russian Federation (2013) it furthermore states that any action which aims to overthrow a legitimate sovereign state, even with the objective to protect the civilian population, is a threat to world peace and stability. Foreign Minister Lavrov (2012, in Allison, 2013: 808) even argues that the Western state's attempt to adopt sanctions against Assad to protect the Syrian population is "a cover for a grand geopolitical game" and that, indeed, "many have in mind not so much Syria as Iran", which is Russia's most important ally in the region (Katz, 2013). This quote demonstrates Russia's distrust in the US which have been working for years against the Iranian government because of its radical Islamist policies but mainly because it denies US ally Israel its right to existence (ibid.). Arguments postulating that the whole region is increasingly destabilised by the ethnic and religious conflict were countered by Lavrov who asserted that this would only happen if the Syrian government collapsed (Aksenyonok, 2013).

Secondly, since the Cold War, in which the USSR attempted to increase its influence in the Middle East, Russia has had an enduring relationship with the Assad regime (Hinnebusch, 2002). Since the 1980s, Russia has had a naval facility, including 40,000 military personnel, in Syria's city Tartus to secure Russia's presence in the region: nowadays this is the only one remaining outside of the former USSR territory and thus important for Russia's geopolitical stance (Katz, 2013). Russia's arms industry has predominately benefitting from the relationship with Syria, since Syria started to purchase Russian weaponry, including chemical missiles, at the beginning of the Cold War and since then has become one of Russia's biggest clients (Hinnebusch, 2002). In other words, Russia's reluctance to lose a long-term political and military supporter in the Middle East explains its continued support for Assad (Allison, 2013).

However, Russia made clear that even though it blocks actions against the Assad regime "Russia's involvement in the armed conflict is out of the question" (Lavrov, 2012 in: Interfax AFN, 2012). Russia's preoccupation with Ukraine since the beginning of 2014 strengthened this position (Engle, 2014). Therefore, Russian policy in the UNSC with regards to Syria can be seen as less ideological and more pragmatic since a lot of Russia's interests are at stake in the case of a Syrian regime change. Consequently, whilst Russia continues to demand a political solution to the conflict, mediated by Russia itself or the UN Special Envoy, without promoting regime change from the outside (Allison, 2013), it also sells weapons to the Syrian regime with which thousands of civilians are killed (Hughes, 2014). As a result, Russia's image in the West and the Middle East is suffering and, with the increasing likelihood of a crumbling Syrian regime, Russia might ultimately face losing an ally in the Middle East, even without military interference from the outside (Allison, 2013).

In contrast to Russia, China has little economic and political interest in Syria and has been relatively even-handed in its dealings with the Syrian government and opposition, for example, by hosting regime and opposition representatives in 2012, and additionally supporting neither the Assad regime nor the opposition in any way (Sun, 2012; Summers, 2013).

The Chinese government has been consistent in all of its statements: the permanent representative, Baodong, justifies his country's position through its firm belief in "state sovereignty, territorial integrity" and respect for the "choices and will of the Syrian people" (UNSC Res. 2042, 2012; UNSC Res. 2043, 2012; UNSC Res. 2139, 2014). This reflects the traditional Chinese principles of diplomacy, namely the "non-intervention in the internal affairs of other states, and a desire for the UN as a collective body to have more authority than individual members" (Summers, 2013). This explains its insistence on a peaceful settlement to the conflict (UNSC Res, 2043, 2012; Res. 2139, 2014). Furthermore, in 2013, China's Foreign Minister Yi stated that the Middle East could not afford another war with external interference since this would destabilise the whole region (Lehman, 2013).

Logically, all of these reasons might lead to abstentions in UNSC Resolutions, but not to a veto. However, China's negative attitude towards an involvement in the internal affairs of another country hardened because of its dissatisfaction with the western led intervention in Libya in 2011 which has a direct impact on its actions regarding Syria today (Lee, 2013). In the Libyan case, China abstained from the UNSC vote and thus made the use of military force under R2P possible. But this did not pay off for the Chinese government because of two main reasons: firstly, it was China who lost the most when the Gaddafi regime collapsed since it lost a traditional ally, including oil deals and arms sales, and has been unable to come to any economic or political agreement with the new Libyan government (Sun, 2012).

Secondly, and more importantly, China's government was severely criticised at home for "compromising its principles [...] and acquiescing to Western demands" (Sun, 2012).

Consequently, China has more to gain than to lose by vetoing in the Syrian case. In so doing, China demonstrates its commitment to its traditional principles of Chinese diplomacy and independence from Western states, but also Sino-Russian diplomatic cooperation which reflects the dedication of China's new leadership to intensifying its relationship with Russia, especially during negotiations for a huge gas deal between the two countries which was signed in June 2014 (Summer, 2013; Topham and Tsukimori, 2014).

The European Union, on the other hand, has been the first to recognise the Syrian National Council as the representative of the Syrian people and to pass sanctions and embargos (The UK government official homepage, 2013). The EU is responsible for sending the most humanitarian aid to the Syrian people and emphasising the need for the UN to support a democratic transition in Syria (European Commission, 2014b). However, the permanent UNSC members, Britain and France, also wanted the EU to demonstrate its support for the Syrian rebels by supplying them with arms (Hughes, 2014). Therefore, both countries voted against the renewal of the arms embargo on Syria in 2013, which divided the EU (Pawlak and Croft, 2013). Nevertheless, both governments have so far denied providing direct military assistance in the forms of weapons and other military equipment (Hughes, 2014).

In 2013, France and the UK wanted to further their support for the Syrian opposition and hence proposed a military intervention to their respective parliaments. Prime Minister Cameron (cited in Cabinet Office, 2013) justified his decision by arguing that Britain could not accept the breach of international law, stating that the vote was not "about getting involved in a Middle Eastern war, or changing our stance in Syria, or going further into that conflict, [...] it's about chemical weapons. Their use is wrong and the world shouldn't stand idly by". However, he failed to get a majority vote in August 2013 since the opposing members of parliament argued that the British population was largely against the involvement of British troops in further overseas conflicts (Winnet, 2013). Since this defeat, Cameron has not proposed military action against the Assad regime again, which could be seen as a sign for his lack of commitment to the use of force in the first place. Instead the government declares that:

> "from outside the country, the UK continues to support transition to a democratic and stable Syria [...]. We are supporting diplomatic efforts that lead to an end to violence and a process of genuine political transition, and investigations into the grave human rights situation. The UK is also providing significant humanitarian assistance inside Syria and to refugees in neighbouring countries" (The UK government official homepage, 2014).

The lack of reference to weaponry supplies and military intervention in this and any other statement since August 2013 shows the government's change of course.

While France has been cooperating closely with Britain and the US, and strongly supported military action against the Syrian regime, the French government especially worked within the UNSC to get authorisation for any measures. French Permanent Representative Araud proposed more drafts than any other representative to the UNSC: while UNSC Resolution 2118 (2013) was approved, the other two failed as a result of vetoes (UNSC 10536, 2012; UNSC Meeting 7180, 2014). France worked on reaching a compromise between the opposing sides in the UNSC by presenting a resolution which, on the one hand, emphasised Syria's territorial integrity but, on the other hand, referred individuals who are known to have violated international law to the ICC (UNSC Meeting 7810, 2014). This shows France's attempt to demonstrate its decisive foreign policy and also to work within the UN's legal and political framework.

However, another reason for France's stance is its long-term, but difficult, relationship with Syria, given it was the former colonial power of Syria and Lebanon (1920- 1946) (Neep, 2012). Khoury (1987) argues that France's uneven rule and interest in its mandate, and additionally its policy of administrative minority enclaves, particularly favouring the Druze and Alawite, provided the grounds for the chaotic internal and external Syrian politics in the first fifteen years of independence with fourteen different presidents. When the French departed Syria in 1946, they left a political vacuum which ultimately made it possible for the Socialist Ba'ath Party to gain power (ibid.). As a result, France is accused of having contributed to Syria's internal social and political tensions which have led to Syria's problem today.

Since the end of the French mandate, Franco- Syrian relationships have been strained, mostly because of Syria's Lebanon policy which is dominated by Syrian's disregard for Lebanese sovereignty, including the Syrian occupation from 1976 to 2004, and its geostrategic interests in the region which resulted in Lebanon becoming the battleground for several proxy wars, including one Israel-Syrian war (Yacoubian, 2006). Additionally, the Assad regime has contributed to the social and political instability in Lebanon by supporting Hezbollah groups and is even suspected of having been involved in the assassination of former Lebanese Prime Minister, Rafik Hariri, in 2005 (ibid.). This has also affected France since Lebanon is its most important political and economic partner in the Middle East (France Diplomatie, 2013). As such, France is the fourth biggest supplier to the Lebanese economy and cooperates extensively with regard to internal security and civil defence (ibid.). Therefore, President Hollande's attempts to solve the conflict and prevent it from spreading further to neighbouring countries also serves France's economic and strategic interests and strengthens France's position in the Middle East. The US were one of the first countries to demand Assad's resignation as president of Syria in August 2011 (Sharp and Blanchard, 2012; Laub and Masters, 2013). President Obama made his fears clear from the beginning that chaos in Syria could provide terrorist organisation al-Qaeda with a safe haven, which would endanger the stability of the whole region and the nation building process in Iraq and Afghanistan (ibid; Landis, 2012). This could ultimately threaten US national security (Obama, 2013). In June 2013, the US government reported that, if the Assad regime were to cross the line and use chemical weapons the US would consider military action (Laub and Masters, 2013).

However, the Obama administration has not been enthusiastic about becoming militarily involved in the Syrian conflict, mostly because it has been attempting to reduce the military presence and costs of the US military in the Middle East for the past years (Allison, 2013). The Obama emphasised that he wants Bashar al Assad out of power, but this demand was only partly motivated by humanitarian concern and largely by the advantage that a collapsed Syrian government would deprive Iran of its most powerful ally in the region (Gwertzman, 2014). If the Syrian civil war were to end with a Sunni leadership, it might, with the Sunni, and US ally, countries Saudi Arabia and Turkey, counterbalance Iran, something which is especially necessary now that Iraq is moving more towards an alliance with Iran (ibid).

Moreover, the US population is extremely war wary: according to a Reuters/Ipsos poll (2013), conducted after the chemical attacks on civilians in Syria in 2013, 96.3% of the Americans surveyed were against the US becoming militarily involved and only 3.7% in favour. In other words, even if the Obama administration decided to undertake military action against Assad's regime, they would face strong opposition from the American public.

This, and the fact that the British parliament rejected its government's notion to join forces with the US in a military intervention (Winnet, 2013), explains why the Obama administration withdrew its proposal to Congress for the authorisation of military action in September 2013 (BBC, 2013); despite some Congress men expressing their approval beforehand, suggesting that "a military presence will position the United States to empower moderates at the expense of extremists" (Laub and Masters, 2013). Instead, alongside the UK and France, Obama has been pushing for collective sanctions in the UNSC and for a smooth transition of power in Syria through diplomatic negotiations (SC/ 10536, 2012; SC/10714, 2012). By the end of 2013, the US government, in cooperation with Saudi Arabia and Qatar, started to send small arms and ammunition to the Syrian opposition, non-affiliated with terrorist groups such as al-Qaeda, and is therefore sustaining the armed conflict (Laub and Masters, 2013).

In summary, on the one hand, the US accuses the "heinous Assad regime and those Member States that refused to join the international community and fellow Security Council members that refused to take firm action against the regime" of being responsible for prolonging the suffering of millions of Syrians (US Permanent Representative to the UNSC Rice, 2012 in SC/10714, 2012). But, on the other hand, the Obama has not acted decisively on his own, changing tact on how and when to react, setting lines for a military intervention but never following through with consequences.

In conclusion, there are signs that Syria is developing into a case of proxy warfare with the permanent members of the UNSC, apart from China which mostly seeks to be neutral. Additionally, Saudi Arabia, Iran and Qatar have been supporting either side of the warring parties (Doyle, 2014). These wars, as demonstrated in Afghanistan at the end of the Cold War, usually suffer from the instigating policy-makers' lack of long-term planning and their obliviousness of, or disinterest in, the implications of their actions (Hughes, 2014). In Afghanistan, for example, the US and other Western states stopped supporting the Mujahedin immediately after the Soviet troops had left Afghan territory in 1989. This resulted in a civil war and the rise of the Taliban and Al-Qaeda's rise (ibid). Back then, the short-term political goals of individual states were prioritised over humanitarian concerns and the need to find an international consensus. The world is still dealing with the consequences.

After the end of the Cold War, the international community's dedication to coordinating their policies, to prioritising human rights, and to fighting mass atrocities raised hopes that R2P becomes state practice. However, the Syrian case proves that the responsibility to stop people's extreme suffering does not lead the decision-making process in the main human rights organisation UN, and thus the international community as a whole. Instead, there is strong evidence that economic and political interests prevail over humanitarian concerns. Syria therefore demonstrates that R2P might promise that basic human rights preside over economic gains and geo-strategic advantages, but, in the end, state practice is still guided by Realpolitik which subordinates R2P.

6   Conclusion

In summary, Legal Doctrinal Research led to the identification of a set of criteria, divided into peaceful and military principles, upon which all members of the UN agreed. Consequently, it has been demonstrated that R2P is more than just a concept: it is a *Jus Cogens* norm and, thus, should guide actions in international relations. The presentation of the Libyan civil war in 2011 furthermore showed that the military aspect of R2P is not only a theoretical concept, but it is used by the UNSC as a basis to make decisions on how to react to mass atrocities. In other words, R2P promises that the international community will not stand by when other human beings' rights are violated to an extreme extent. Therefore, the UN's reaction to the Syrian civil war is so difficult to understand since the UNSC has been acting contrarily to its commitment.

Hence, the case study on Syria has confirmed the threefold premise postulated in the introduction. Firstly, the situation in Syria indeed falls within the scope of R2P with its extreme scale of violence and human suffering caused by all conflict parties. Therefore, it is the international community's responsibility to act and protect the Syrian population from the perpetrators, be they opposition or government forces.

Secondly, the analysis indicated that the UN has failed to fulfil its R2P towards the Syrian population since it has not exhausted all its available instruments to prevent the conflict from escalating, and has not reacted to the considerable human rights abuse. The UN took too long to decide how to react and thus missed the window of opportunity during which the situation had been evolving but had not developed yet into an armed conflict. When the UNSC finally were able to find a consensus and created the position of the Special Envoy of the UN and the Arab League, it did not reinforce its efforts by threatening the Syrian regime and the opposition with consequences for non-compliance. Even though some regional organisations and individual states tried to compensate the UNSC's lack of consensus by passing their own sanctions, these were not successful since other states, such as Russia, simultaneously supported the regime. A true isolation of the regime and opposition groups might have forced the warring parties to make concessions at the negotiation table. However, the UNSC was unable to agree on these. In conclusion, the Six Point Peace Plan and all attempts to mediate and stop the violence by sending unarmed observers were doomed to fail from the beginning because of the lack of accountability.

As a consequence of the UN's inability to fulfil its responsibility to prevent and to react, the situation in Syria today seems to have escalated beyond the point of political negotiations. The opposition groups are fighting against each other and the Assad regime, and all groups are known to violate IHL and deny civilians even the most basic human rights. They thus contradict everything the UN stands for and R2P intends to prevent or stop.

An investigation of the conditions for the use of force under R2P in Syria has revealed that the *Just Cause* threshold has been met since there is strong evidence of war crimes and crimes against humanity. Furthermore, the use of force constitutes *Last Resort* since further diplomatic efforts, in the unlikely case that the UN would be able to agree on any, are likely to fail "because diplomacy always reflects the power relationship on the ground" (Abrams, 2014). The reason for this is that the opposition groups and the Assad regime have been unable to find a compromise in the last three years. The fact that even the most experienced diplomats, Annan and Brahimi, failed to influence the behaviour of all participants in any way further indicates the unlikeliness of diplomatic success in the near future. Instead, it seems as if the situation has reached a stalemate.

Moreover, the situation in Syria is no longer only affecting the Syrian population anymore but is equally endangering the stability of the whole Middle East. Countries such as Lebanon and Jordan are struggling with the refugee influx from Syria and have to bear the economic and social consequences of a chaotic, warring neighbouring state. Accordingly, the Middle Eastern countries' ability to fulfil their R2P towards their own citizens but also towards the Syrians is severely affected. The current situation in Iraq, with extremist organisation ISIS controlling a large part of Iraq's northern territory and committing serious human rights violations, is a result of the civil war in Syria since it provides Islamist terrorist with a safe haven. Therefore, this degenerating civil war in Syria has become a *Threat to International Peace and Security*. In summary, the Syrian civil war fulfils all conditions for the use of force under R2P which validates a reaction by the UNSC to the massive human rights violations in Syria. However, the lack of consensus in the UNSC makes it unlikely that the UNSC will ever enforce the military instruments of R2P.

The Syrian case thirdly demonstrates the practical ineffectiveness of R2P and that state interests still prevail over the responsibility to protect strangers. R2P does not require policymakers to ignore their own state's interest while reacting towards strangers. Nonetheless, R2P is based on the assumption that policymakers weigh up their options and prioritise human rights over their economic and geo-strategic interests. However, this study indicates that the permanent fives' motives to propose action against the Syrian regime, or the opposition, or veto any action at all, is largely motivated either by the fact that they would benefit from one party's victory, for example, in the case of Russia or the US, or because there is no gain at all in becoming involved, such as for China. Also, economic interest or the attempt to prove alliance to a specific country by voting in its favour seems to be a deciding factor. Hence, the permanent five have been individually supporting one side of the conflict and thus contributing to the increasing scale of violence and the resulting chaos within Syria, at Syria's neighbours' borders, and increasingly in Iraq, instead of focusing on the suffering of the Syrian civilians. However, it is important to note that even though individual states are willing to send weapons, money and humanitarian aid to one side of the conflict, they have shown no interest in becoming militarily involved. This could be the result of the lack of national support in the Western states for military action in another Middle Eastern conflict, and also the West's and Russia's preoccupation elsewhere, respectively Iraq and Ukraine.

In conclusion, this study demonstrated that Syria is only a part of a broader construct. R2P is still a theoretical concept, despite being practiced in the Libyan case and its implementation in international law. R2P might promise that basic human rights prevail over economic gains and geo-strategic advantages, but, in the end, Realpolitik prevails over humanitarian concerns. Therefore, R2P cannot practice what it promises or, in other words, the UN cannot practice what it promises. If member states even refuse to vote in favour of sanctions because it is against their national interests, in spite of being signatory to a *Jus Cogens* norm theoretically condemning the actions of a sanctioned state, it damages the credibility of the UN. On the one hand, this will result in rogue states and militias in Syria and other parts of the world continuing to commit mass murder, sexual violence and torture without fear of the consequences. On the other hand, it means that the UN is not able to defend its own core principles, which makes the UN a powerless organisation.

Ultimately, the debate on R2P is unfinished: while the Syrians have to suffer from the consequences of the international community's lack of commitment to help them, the UN itself must consider changes in its decision making process or even has to redefine itself. There are various possibilities how to solve the dilemma of a UNSC deadlock, among others the ICISS's proposal to allow the GA to act in place of the UNSC if the latter fails to fulfil its R2P. However, this discussion is not new and is unlikely to be solved in the near future. And, more importantly, it is unlikely to force states to prioritise human rights over state interests. Nevertheless, the UN has to decide which role it wants to play in humanitarian disasters. It might be that the commitment to R2P had been too ambitious for an organisation that consists of a multitude of independent states, especially since the concept itself is still perceived as western by China and Russia. In this case, the UN has to reconsider its capability limitations and might have to return to solely promoting human rights, and forsake defending and protecting the human rights of all individuals. Meanwhile, the search for a consensus on how to help the Syrian population must continue.

Appendix

Table 1: Comparison of the ICISS' R2P criteria with R2P implementation in international law and UNSC documents

R2P2001 (ICISS, 2001)	RtoP incorporated in international treaties, resolutions, laws	Written down in
Primary responsibility to protect a state's populations lies with the state, if "the state in question is unwilling or unable to halt or avert it, the principle of non-intervention yields to the international responsibility to protect" (p. 10)	States have the responsibility to protect the population, The international community has to support states to fulfil this responsibility and has to step in, if these fail to fulfil their responsibility	2005 World Summit Outcome Document § 138, 139, reaffirmed in UNSC Res. 1674
Responsibility to prevent: Addresses both the root causes and direct causes of internal conflict and other man-made crisis (p.22f)	"This responsibility entails the prevention of such crimes, including their incitement, through appropriate and necessary means."	2005 World Summit Outcome Document, § 138,
	"We also intend to commit ourselves, as necessary and appropriate, to helping States build capacity to protect their populations from genocide, war crimes, ethnic cleansing and crimes against humanity and to assisting those which are under stress before crises and conflicts break out."	§ 139
	"[...] to take such action under the Charter of the United Nations as they consider appropriate for the prevention and suppression of acts of genocide or any of the other acts enumerated in Article 3"	Genocide Convention § 8
Responsibility to react To respond to situation of compelling human need with appropriate measures, which include coercive measures such as sanctions, international prosecution, and at last resort military action (p.29ff)	"the international community, through the United Nations, also has the responsibility to use appropriate diplomatic, humanitarian and other peaceful means, in accordance with Chapters VI and VIII of the Charter, to help protect populations **from genocide, war crimes, ethnic cleansing and crimes against humanity.**"	2005 World Summit Outcome Document, § 139
Responsibility to rebuild To provide, particularly after a	Establishment of Peacebuilding Commission	General Assembly Res. A/RES/60/180 on the

military intervention, full assistance with recovery, reconstruction and reconciliation, addressing the causes of the harm the intervention was designed to stop or avert (p.39ff)	" [...]Recognizing also the vital role of the United Nations in preventing conflicts, assisting parties of conflicts to end hostilities and emerge towards recovery, reconstruction and development and in mobilizing sustained international attention and assistance, [...]"	20th of December 2005 Adopted by the UNSC in S/RES/1645 on the 20th of December 2005
Criteria for military intervention (p.31-39)	No criteria ➔ case to case basis Threat must be to international peace and security for the UNSC to authorize the use of force UNSC acknowledges a direct correlation between the protection of civilians and potential threats to international peace and security "notes that the deliberate targeting of civilian populations [...] and the committing of systematic, flagrant and widespread violations of international humanitarian and human rights law in situation of armed conflict may constitute a threat to international peace and security, and, in this regard reaffirms its readiness to consider such situations and, where necessary, to adopt appropriate measures"	World Summit Document Outcome 2005 § 139 UN Charter Chapter VII, Article 24 UN Charter UNSC Res. 1296, 19th April 2000
1. **Just cause** (p.32) • Large scale loss of life (actual or apprehended) • Large scale ethnic cleansing	• Genocide • War crimes • Ethnic cleansing • Crimes against humanity Threat to international peace and security	2005 World Summit Outcome Document § 138, 139, reaffirmed in UNSC Res. 1674 UN Charter Chapter VII, Article 24, UN Charter
2. **Right authority** (p.35) UNSC primarily, if not able to react in a timely and decisive manner, regional organisations can react	Security Council as the only body to authorize the use of force according to Chapter VII of the Charter and IHL **BUT!** Cooperation with regional organisation	World Summit Outcome Document § 139 UN Charter Chapter VII

3. **Last resort** (p.31)	"we are prepared to take collective action, in a timely and decisive manner, through the Security Council [...] should peaceful means be inadequate and national authorities manifestly fail to protect their populations from genocide, war crimes, ethnic cleansing and crimes against humanity.	2005 World Summit Outcome Document § 139
	"[...] that measure provided for in Article 41 proved to be inadequate, it may take such action by air, sea, or land forces as may be necessary to maintain or restore international peace and security"	Chapter VII of the Charter § 42
4. **Proportionality** (p.35)	"it [Security Council] may take such action by air, sea, or land forces as may be necessary to maintain or restore international peace and security"	Chapter VII of the Charter § 42
5. **Reasonable Prospects**(p.35)		
6. **Right Intention** (p.35)		

Table 2: R2P References in United Nations Security Council Resolutions and Presidential Statements

Resolutions

Date	Document #	Situation or Issue	Text
27 January 2006	S/RES/1653	DRC and Burundi	"*Underscores* that the governments in the region have a primary responsibility to protect their populations,"
28 April 2006	S/RES/1674	POC	"*Reaffirms* the provisions of paragraphs 138 and 139 of the 2005 World Summit Outcome Document regarding the responsibility to protect populations from genocide, war crimes, ethnic cleansing and crimes against humanity;"
31 August 2006	S/RES/1706	Sudan (Darfur)	"*Recalling also* its previous resolutions 1325 (2000) on women, peace and security, 1502 (2003) on the protection of humanitarian and United Nations personnel, 1612 (2005) on children and armed conflict, and 1674 (2006) on the protection of civilians in armed conflict, which reaffirms inter alia the provisions of paragraphs 138 and 139 of the 2005 United Nations World Summit outcome document,"
11 November 2009	S/RES/1894	POC	"*Reaffirming* the relevant provisions of the 2005 World Summit Outcome Document regarding the protection of civilians in armed conflict, including paragraphs 138 and 139 thereof regarding the responsibility to protect populations from genocide, war crimes, ethnic cleansing and crimes against humanity,"
26 February 2011	S/RES/1970	Libya	"*Recalling* the Libyan authorities' responsibility to protect its population,"
17 March 2011	S/RES/1973	Libya	"*Reiterating* the responsibility of the Libyan authorities to protect the Libyan population and reaffirming that parties to armed conflicts bear the primary responsibility to take all feasible steps to ensure the protection of civilians,"
30 March 2011	S/RES/1975	Côte d'Ivoire	"...*reaffirming* the primary responsibility of each State to protect civilians and reiterating that parties to armed conflicts bear the primary responsibility to take all feasible steps to ensure the protection of civilians..."
8 July 2011	S/RES/1996	South Sudan	"Advising and assisting the Government of the Republic of South Sudan, including military and police at national and local levels as appropriate, in fulfilling its responsibility to protect civilians,"
21 October 2011	S/RES/2014	Yemen	"*Recalling* the Yemeni Government's primary responsibility to protect its population,"

27 October 2011	S/RES/2016	Libya	"...*underscores* the Libyan authorities' responsibility for the protection of its population, including foreign nationals and African migrants;"
12 March 2012	S/RES/2040	Libya	"...underscores the Libyan authorities' primary responsibility for the protection of Libya's population,"
19 December 2012	S/RES/2085	Mali	"(d) To support the Malian authorities in their primary responsibility to protect the population;"
6 March 2013	S/RES/2093	Somalia	"*Recognizing* that the Federal Government of Somalia has a responsibility to protect its citizens and build its own national security forces,"
12 March 2013	S/RES/2095	Libya	"...*underscores* the Libyan government's primary responsibility for the protection of Libya's population, as well as foreign nationals, including African migrants;"
25 April 2013	S/RES/2100	Mali	"*Reiterates* that the transitional authorities have the primary responsibility to protect civilians in Mali,"
11 July 2013	S/RES/2109	Sudan/South Sudan	"*Recalling* the Presidential Statement of 12 February 2013 that recognized that States bear the primary responsibility to protect civilians as well as to respect and ensure the human rights of all individuals within their territory and subject to their jurisdiction as provided for by relevant international law, reaffirmed that parties to armed conflict bear the primary responsibility to take all feasible steps to ensure the protection of civilians, urged parties to armed conflict to meet civilians' basic needs, and condemned all violations of international law against civilians, in particular the deliberate targeting of civilians, indiscriminate or disproportionate attacks, and sexual and gender based violence."
26 September 2013	S/RES/2117	Small Arms and Light Weapons	"*Recognizing that* the misuse of small arms and light weapons has resulted in grave crimes and *reaffirming* therefore the relevant provisions of the 2005 World Summit Outcome Document regarding the protection of civilians in armed conflict, including paragraphs 138 and 139 thereof regarding the responsibility to protect populations from genocide, war crimes, ethnic cleansing and crimes against humanity,"
10 October 2013	S/RES/2121	Central African Republic	"*Underscores* the primary responsibility of the Central African authorities to protect the population"
5 December 2013	S/RES/2127	Central African Republic	"*Recalling* that the Transitional Authorities have the primary responsibility to protect the civilian population," "*Underscores* the primary responsibility of the Transitional Authorities to protect the population,"
28 January 2014	S/RES/2134	Central African Republic	"*Recalling* that the Transitional Authorities have the primary responsibility to protect the civilian population in the CAR,"
22 February 2014	S/RES/2139	Syria	"Also demands that all parties take all appropriate steps to protect civilians, including members of ethnic, religious and confessional

			communities, and stresses that, in this regard, the primary responsibility to protect its population lies with the Syrian authorities;"
10 April 2014	S/RES/2149	Central African Republic	"*Recalling* that the Transitional Authorities have the primary responsibility to protect the civilian population in the CAR,"
16 April 2014	S/RES/2150	Threats to International Peace and Security	"*Recognizing* that States bear the primary responsibility to respect and ensure the human rights of their citizens, as well as other individuals within their territory as provided for by relevant international law, *Acknowledging* the important role played by regional and subregional arrangements in the prevention of, and response to, situations that may lead to genocide, war crimes and crimes against humanity, especially noting Article 4(h)of the Constitutive Act of the African Union, *Recalling the important role of the Secretary-General's* Special Advisers on the Prevention of Genocide and the Responsibility to Protect, whose functions include acting as an early warning mechanism to prevent potential situations that could result in genocide, crimes against humanity, war crimes and ethnic cleansing," "*Calls upon* States to recommit to prevent and fight against genocide, and other serious crimes under international law, *reaffirms* paragraphs 138 and 139 of the 2005 World Summit Outcome Document (A/60/L.1) on the responsibility to protect populations from genocide, war crimes, ethnic cleansing and crimes against humanity, and *underscores* the importance of taking into account lessons learned from the 1994 Genocide against the Tutsi in Rwanda, during which Hutu and others who opposed the genocide were also killed;"

Presidential Statements

Year	Document #	Situation or Issue	Text
22 September 2011	S/PRST/2011/18	Maintenance of international peace and security	"reaffirms the responsibility of each individual State to protect its populations from genocide, war crimes, ethnic cleansing, and crimes against humanity"
14 November 2011	S/PRST/2011/21	Central Africa (LRA)	"The Security Council underlines the primary responsibility of States in the LRA-affected region to protect civilians and calls upon them to take all appropriate measures in this regard."
29 June 2012	S/PRST/2012/18	Central Africa (LRA)	"The Security Council underlines the primary responsibility of States in the LRA-affected region to protect civilians and calls upon them to take all appropriate measures in this regard."
19 December 2012	S/PRST/2012/28	Central Africa (LRA)	"The Security Council underlines the primary responsibility of States in the LRA-affected region to protect civilians and calls upon them to

			take all appropriate measures in this regard."
12 February 2013	S/PRST/2013/2	Protection of Civilians in Armed Conflict	"The Security Council recognizes that States bear the primary responsibility to protect civilians" ... "The Security Council reaffirms the relevant provisions of the 2005 World Summit Outcome Document regarding the protection of civilians in armed conflict, including paragraphs 138 and 139 thereof regarding the responsibility to protect populations from genocide, war crimes, ethnic cleansing and crimes against humanity"
15 April 2013	S/PRST/2013/4	Peace and Security in Africa	"The Council underlines the importance of raising awareness of and ensuring respect of all applicable international law, including international humanitarian law and human rights law, stresses the importance of the responsibility to protect as outlined in the 2005 World Summit outcome document, including the primary responsibility of Member States to protect their populations from genocide, ethnic cleansing, crimes against humanity and war crimes. The Council further underlines the role of the international community in encouraging and helping States, including through capacity-building, to meet their primary responsibility. The Council looks forward to the 2013 UN Secretary-General report on the Responsibility to Protect. The Council further recalls the important role of the Secretary-General's Special Advisers on the Prevention of Genocide and Responsibility to Protect in matters relating to the prevention and resolution of conflict."
17 June 2013	S/PRST/2013/8	Children and Armed Conflict	"The Security Council stresses that ending impunity and holding perpetrators accountable is a crucial element in halting and preventing violations and abuses committed against children and recalls the primary responsibility of States in that regard, including to hold accountable those responsible for genocide, crimes against humanity, war crimes and other egregious crimes perpetrated against children."
2 October 2013	S/PRST/2013/15	Middle East	"The Council recalls in this regard that the Syrian authorities bear the primary responsibility to protect their populations."
12 February 2014	S/PRST/2014/3	Protection of Civilians in Armed Conflict	"The Security Council recalls that States bear the primary responsibility to respect and ensure the human rights of their citizens, as well as all individuals within their territory as provided for by relevant international law and reaffirms the responsibility of each individual State to protect its populations from genocide, war crimes, ethnic cleansing, and crimes against humanity."

Source: Global Centre for the Responsibility to Protect. (2014). Retrieved from: http://www.globalr2p.org/media/files/unsc-resolutions-and-statements-with-r2p-table-as-of-august-2014.pdf (accessed 27/8/2014)

Bibliography

1. Primary Sources

1.1. UN Documents

Additional Protocol to the Geneva Conventions. (1977, June 6). *Protocol Additional I to the Geneva Conventions of 12 August 1949, and relating to the Protection of Victims of International Armed Conflict (Protocol I).* Retrieved from: https://treaties.un.org/doc/Publication/UNTS/Volume%201125/volume-1125-I-17512-English.pdf (accessed 08/08/2014)

Annan, K. (2000). *We the People: The Role of the United Nations in the 21st Century.* Retrieved from United Nations Millenium Report:http://www.un.org/millenium/sg/report/full.html (accessed 25/5/2014)

Brahimi, L. (2013). *Interview with UN-Arab League Joint Special Representative for Syria, Lakhdar Brahimi.* UN Department of Political Affairs. Retrieved from: http://www.un.org/wcm/content/site/undpa/main/enewsletter/pid/24721 (accessed 06/06/2014)

Convention on the Prevention and Punishment of the Crime of Genocide (Genocide Convention) (1948, December 9). New York, United States: United Nations Document Service.

International Commission on Intervention and State Sovereignty. (2001). *The Responsibility to Protect.* Ottawa, Canada: IDRC.

Independent Commission of Inquiry on Libya (2011, June). A/HRC/17/44. *Report of the International Commission of Inquiry to investigate all alleged violations of international human rights law in the Libyan Arab Jamahiriya.* New York, United States: Report of the Human Rights Council.

Independent International Commission of Inquiry on the Syrian Arab Republic First Report (2011, November 23). A/HRC/S-17/2/Add.1. Retrieved from: http://daccess-ddsny.un. org/doc/UNDOC/GEN /G11/170 /97/PDF/G1117097.pdf?OpenElement (accessed 20/5/2014)

Independent International Commission of Inquiry on the Syrian Arab Republic Third Report (2012, February 22). A/HRC/19/69. Retrieved from: http://daccess-ddsny.un.org /doc/UNDOC/GEN/G12/106/13/PDF/G1210613.pdf?OpenElement (accessed 20/5/2014)

United Nations Department of Political Affairs. (2014). *Interview with UN-Arab League Joint Special Representative for Syria, Lakhdar Brahimi.* Retrieved from the Homepage of the United Nations Department of Political Affairs: http://www.un.org/wcm/content/site/undpa/main/ enewsletter/pid/24721 (accessed 02/07/2014)

United Nations Human Rights Council Resolution A/HRC/14/44. (2011, February 25). New York, United States: Report of the Human Rights Council.

United Nations Human Rights Council Resolution A/HRC/S-16/2. (2011, April 29). Retrieved from:http://www.ohchr.org/Documents/HRBodies/HRCouncil/SpecialSession/Session16/A-HRC-S-16-2.pdfNew York, United States (accessed 20/7/2014)

United Nations Human Rights Council Resolution A/HRC/S-17/2. (2011, August 22). Retrieved
from: http://daccess-ddsny.un.org/doc/UNDOC/GEN/G11/169/88/PDF/G1116988.pdf?OpenElement (accessed 20/7/2014)

UNHCR. (2011, March). *UNHCR Supplementary Budget: The Libya Situation 2011.* Retrieved from UNCHR The UN Refugee Agency: http://www.unhcr.org/4d710ad49.pdf (accessed 2/6/2014)

UNHCR. (2014, August). *Syria Regional Refugee Response.* Retrieved from UNHCR The UN Refugee Agency: http://data.unhcr.org/syrianrefugees/regional.php (accessed 01/08/2014)

UN Mission to Investigate Allegations of the Use of Chemical Weapons in the Syrian Arab Republic. (2013, August 21). *Report on the Alleged Use of Chemical Weapons in the Ghouta Area of Damascus.* Retrieved from: http://www.un.org/disarmament/content/slideshow/Secretary_General_Report_of_CW_Investigation.pdf (accessed 03/05/2014)

United Nations News Centre. (2011, December 12). *As Syrian death toll tops 5,000, UN human rights chief warns about key city.* Retrieved from United Nations News Centre: http://www.un.org/apps/news/story.asp?NewsID=40708#.U9tTqvl5OoE (accessed 30/7/2014)

United Nations News Centre. (2014, May 13). *Syria: UN-Arab League envoy Brahimi resigns.* Retrieved from United Nations News Centre : http://www.un.org/apps/news/story.asp?NewsID=47780#.U9tV_fl5OoE (accessed 15/5/2014)

United Nations Security Council Resolution 1645 (2005, December 12). S/RES/1645. Retrieved from: http://daccess-dds-ny.un.org/doc/UNDOC/GEN/N05/654/17/PDF/N0565417.pdf? OpenElement (accessed 6/7/2014)

United Nation Security Council Resolution 1674 (2006, April 28). S/RES/1674. Retrieved from http://daccess-ddsny.un.org/doc/UNDOC/GEN/N06/331/99/PDF/N0633199.pdf? OpenElement (accessed 1/5/2014)

United Nations Security Council Resolution 1970 (2011, February 28). S/RES/1970. Retrieved from: http://daccess-ddsny.un.org/doc/UNDOC/GEN/N11/245/58/PDF/N1124558. pdf? OpenElement

United Nations Security Council Resolution 1973. (2011, March 17). S/RES/1973. Retrieved from:http://www.nato.int/nato_static/assets/pdf/pdf_2011_03/20110927_110311-UNSCR-1973.pdf (accessed 1/4/2014)

United Nations Security Council Resolution 2042. (2012, April 14). S/RES/2042. Retrieved from:http://www.securitycouncilreport.org/atf/cf/%7B65BFCF9B-6D27-4E9C-8CD3-CF6E4FF96FF9%7D/Syria%20SRES%202042.pdf (accessed 20/7/2014)

United Nations Security Council Resolution 2043. (2012, April 21). S/RES/2043. Retrieved from:http://www.securitycouncilreport.org/atf/cf/%7B65BFCF9B-6D27-4E9C-8CD3-CF6E4FF96FF9%7D/Syria%20SRES%202043.pdf (accessed 02/7/2014)

United Nations Security Council Resolution 2059. (2012, July 20). S/RES/2059. Retrieved from: http://www.securitycouncilreport.org/atf/cf/%7B65BFCF9B-6D27-4E9C-8CD3-CF6E4 FF96FF9%7D/Syria%20SRES%202059.pdf (accessed 20/7/2014)

United Nations Security Council Resolution 2118. (2013, September 27). S/RES/2118. Retrieved from:http://www.securitycouncilreport.org/atf/cf/%7B65BFCF9B-6D27-4E9C-8CD3-CF6E4FF9 6FF9% 7D/s_res_2118.pdf (accessed 12/7/2014)

United Nations Security Council Resolution 2139. (2014, February 22). S/RES/2139. Retrieved from: http://www.securitycouncilreport.org/atf/cf/%7B65BFCF9B-6D27-4E9C-8CD3-CF6E4F F96FF9%7D/s_res_2139.pdf (accessed 20/7/2014)

United Nations Security Council Resolution 2150. (2014, April 16). S/RES/2150. Retrieved from:http://www.un.org/en/ga/search/view_doc.asp?symbol=S/RES/2150(2014) (accessed 20/7/2014)

United Nations Security Council Resolution 2169. (2014, July 30). S/Res.2169. Retrieved from: http://unscr.com/en/resolutions/doc/2169 (accessed 11/08/2014)

United Nations Security Council Resolution Draft 10403. (2011, October 4). SC/10403. Retrieved from: http://www.un.org/News/Press/docs/2011/sc10403.doc.htm (accessed 20/7/2014)

United Nations Security Council Resolution Draft 10536. (2012, February 4). SC/10536. Retrieved from: http://www.un.org/News/Press/docs/2012/sc10536.doc.htm (accessed 20/7/2014)

United Nations Security Council Resolution Draft 10714. (2012, July 19). SC/10714. Retrieved from: http://www.un.org/News/Press/docs/2012/sc10714.doc.htm (accessed 20/7/2014)

United Nations Security Council 7180 Meeting. (2014, May 11). S./PV.7180. Retrieved from: http://www.securitycouncilreport.org/atf/cf/%7B65BFCF9B-6D27-4E9C-8CD3-CF6E4 FF96FF9%7D/s_pv_7180.pdf (accessed 20/7/2014)

United Nations Supervision Mission in Syria UNSMIS. (2012, August). Retrieved from: http://www.un.org/en/peacekeeping/missions/unsmis/mandate.shtml (accessed 01/8/2014)

UN Secretary Report to the UNSC on Children and Armed Conflict in Syria. S/2014/31. (2014, January 27). Retrieved from: http://www.un.org/en/ga/search/view_doc.asp?symbol = S/2014/31 (accessed 03/06/2014)

World Summit Outcome Document. A/RES/60/1. (2005, October 25) Retrieved from: http://www.unrol.org/files/2005%20World%20Summit%20Outcome.pdf (accessed 1/5/2014)

1.2. Publications and Statements of States and Regional Organisations

Cabinet Office. (2013, August 27). *Syria: transcript of PM's interview.* Government of the United Kingdom. Retrieved from: https://www.gov.uk/government/speeches/syria-transcript-of-pms-interview (accessed 26/07/2014)

Russian Federation. (2013, February 12). *Concept of the Foreign Policy of the Russian Federation Approved by President of the Russian Federation V. Putin.* Retrieved from: http://www.mid.ru/brp_4.nsf/0/76389FEC168189ED44257B2E0039B16D (accessed 03/07/2014)

European Commission. (2014a, June 26). *Factsheet Syria Crisis.* Retrieved from: http://ec.europa.eu/echo/files/aid/countries/factsheets/syria_en.pdf (accessed 03/05/2014)

European Commission. (2014b, July 8). *Humanitarian Aid and Civil Protection Syria: Three Years of Suffering.* Retrieved from: http://ec.europa.eu/echo/en/where/middle-east-north-africa/syria (accessed 07/08/2014)

France Diplomatie. (2013). Lebanon. Retrieved from: http://www.diplomatie.gouv.fr/en/ country-files/ lebanon-294/ (accessed 01/08/2014)

The UK Government official homepage. (2013, June 4). *Information on embargoes on Syria and how to apply for an export licence.* Retrieved from the Department for Business,

Innovation & Skills, Foreign & Commonwealth Office and Export Control Organisation: https://www.gov.uk/sanctions-on-syria (accessed 20/6/2014)

The UK Government official homepage (2013). *UK and Syria.* Retrieved from: https://www.gov. uk/ government/world/Syria (accessed 12/07/2014)

Obama, B. (2013, September 10). *Remarks by the President in Address to the Nation on Syria.* The White House. Retrieved from: http://www.whitehouse.gov/the-press-office/2013/09/10/remarks-president-address-nation-syria (accessed 01/08/2014)

United States Treasury Department. (2012, May). *Presidential Documents.* Retrieved from US Department of the Treasury Official Homepage: http://www.treasury.gov/resource-center/sanctions/Programs/Documents/fse_eo.pdf (accessed 30/8/2014)

1.3. Non-Governmental Organisation's Publications

Amnesty Internationl. (2013, October). *Growing Restrictions, Tough Conditions: The Plight of Those Fleeing Syria To Jordan.* Retrieved from: http://www.amnestyusa.org/research/reports/growing-restrictions-tough-conditions-the-plight-of-those-fleeing-syria-to-jordan retrieved on 21/11/2013

Amnesty International. (2014a, March 10). *Syria: Yarmouk under siege - a horror story of war crimes, starvation and death.* Retrieved from: http://www.amnesty.org/ en/news/ syria-yarmouk-under-siege-horror-story-war-crimes-starvation-and-death-2014-03-10 (accessed 06/06/2014)

Amnesty International. (2014b, April 17). Syria: *A Country under Siege.* Retrieved from: http://www.amnesty.org.nz/news/syria-country-under-siege (accessed 01/04/2014)

Genocide Watch. (2012, February). *Genocide and Mass Atrocities Alert: Syria.* Retrieved from: http://www.genocidewatch.org/syria.html (accessed 07/07/2014)

Human Rights Watch. (2012). *World Report 2012.* New York, United States: Human Rights Watch.

Human Rights Watch. (2013). *Syria: Criminal Justice for Serious Crimes under International Law.* New York, United States: Human Righst Watch Publishing .

Human Rights Watch. (2014, May 22). *UN Security Council: Vetoes Betray Syrian Victims.* Retrieved from Human Rights Watch News: http://www.hrw.org/news/2014/05/22/ un-security-council-vetoes-betray-syrian-victims (accessed 02/07/2014)

International Committee of the Red Cross. ICRC. (2011). *International Customary Law Study. Rule 156: Definition of War Crimes.* Retrieved from: http://www.icrc.org/customary-ihl/eng/docs/v1_cha_chapter44_rule156 (accessed 27/5/2014)

International Crisis Group. (2011). *Popular Protest in North Africa and the Middle East: The Syrian Regime's a Slow-Motion Suicide.* Brussels, Belgium: International Crisis Group Middle East/North Africa Report No. 109

ICRtoP. (2014 , May). *International Coalition for the Responsibility to Protect* . Retrieved from: http://www.responsibilitytoprotect.org/index.php/crises/crisis-in-syria (accessed 7/7/2014)

World Food Programme. (2014, June 11). Syria Crisis Response Situation Update. Retrieved from:http://documents.wfp.org/stellent/groups/public/documents/ep/wfp266163.pdf (accessed 01/08/2014)

1.4. Polls

Reuters/Ipsos Poll. (2013, September). *US response to possible chemical attacks in Syria: Invade with America troops.* Retrieved from: http://polling.reuters.com/#!response/TM121Y13_5 /type/day/dates/20130822-20130917 (accessed 01/08/2014)

2. Secondary Sources

Abrams, E. (2014, June 13). *Syria: Humanitarian Disaster and Security Threat.* Retrieved from Council on Foreign Relations: http://www.cfr.org/syria/syria-humanitarian-disaster-security-threat/p33082 (accessed 03/06/2014)

Ajami, F. (2012, March). *The Arab Spring at One: A Year of Living Dangerously.* Retrieved from Foreign Affairs: http://www.foreignaffairs.com/articles/137053/fouad-ajami/the-arab-spring-at-one (accessed 25/5/2014)

Aksenyonok, A. (2013, April 15). *Syria As a Mirror of the Changing World Order.* Retrieved from Russia in Global Affairs: http://eng.globalaffairs.ru/number/Syria-As-a-Mirror-of-the-Changing-World-Order-15932 (accessed 01/08/2014)

Al-Akhbar, K. (2014, June 12). *The war in Syria: ISIS's most successful investment yet.* Retrieved from The Syrian Observer: http://syrianobserver.com/Features/Features/The+war+in+Syria+ISISs+most+successful+investment+yet (accessed 07/0/72014)

Allison, R. (2013 , December). Russia and Syria: Explaining Alignment with a Regime in Crisis. *International Affairs, Vol. 89 No. 4* , pp. 795-823.

Anderson, L. (2011, May). *Demystifying the Arab Spring.* Retrieved from Foreign Affairs: http://www.foreignaffairs.com/articles/67693/lisa-anderson/demystifying-the-arab-spring (accessed 28/3/2014)

Arthurs, H. (1983). *Law and Learning: Report to the Social Sciences and Humanities Research Council of Canada by the Consultative Group on Research and Education in Law.* Ottowa, Canada: Information Division, Social Sciences and Humanities Research Council of Canada .

Ayoob, M. (2004, March). Third World Perspectives on Humanitarian Intervention and International Administration. *Global Governance Vol. 10 No.1*, pp. 99-118.

Bajoria, J., & McMahon, R. (2013, June 12). *The Dilemma of Humanitarian Intervention .* Retrieved from Council on Foreign Relations: http://www.cfr.org/humanitarian-intervention/dilemma-humanitarian-intervention/p16524 (accessed 01/05/2014)

Barry, C., & Southwood, N. (2011, March). What is special about human rights? *Ethics and International Affairs, Vol. 25, No. 3*, pp. 369-383.

BBC. (2013, September 11). *Syria crisis: Barack Obama puts military strike on hold.* Retrieved from BBC News: http://www.bbc.co.uk/news/world-us-canada-24043751 (accessed 01/08/2014)

Bellamy, A. (2009). *Responsibility to Protect: The Global Effort to End Mass Atrocities.* Cambridge, United Kingdom: Polity Press.

Bellamy, A. (2011, September). Libya and the Responsibility to Protect: The Excpetion and the Norm. *Ethics and International Affairs Vol.25 Issue 03*, p. 263.269.

Breakey, H. (2012). The Responsibility to Protect and the Protection of Civilians in Armed Conflicts: Overlap and Contrast. In C. Sampford, A. Francis, & V. Popovsk, *Normsof Protection: Responsibility to Protect, Protection of Civilians and Their Interaction* (pp. 62-81). Geneva, Switzerland: United Nations University.

Breau, S. (2005). *Humanitarian Intervention: The United Nations and Collective Responsibiity.* London, United Kingdom: Cameron May Ltd.

Bull, H. (1977). *The Anarchical Society. A Study of Order in World Politics.* New York, United States: Palgrave.

Buzan, B. (2004). *From International to World Society? English School Theory and the Social Structure of Globalisation.* Cambridge, United Kingdom: Cambridge University Press.

Carter, H., & Ehtheshami, A. (2004). *The Middle East's Relations with Asia and Russia.* London, United Kingdom: RoutledgeCurzon.

Chandler, D. (2009). Unravelling the Paradox of the Responsibility to Protect. *Irish Studies in International Affairs Vol.20 No.1*, pp. 27-39.

Chulov, M. (2013, September 30). *Syrian jihadists wreak havoc as violence spreads into Iraq.* Retrieved from The Guardian: http://www.theguardian.com/world/2013/sep/30/syrian-jihadists-wreak-havoc-violence-iraq (accessed 02/07/2014)

Cooker, C. (2001). *Human Warfare.* Oxon, United Kingdom: Routledge.

Council on Foreign Relations. (2012, February 13). *UN High Commissioner for Human Rights'*
Statement on Syria. Retrieved from http://www.cfr.org/syria/un-high-commissioner-
human-rights-statement-syria-february-2012/p27370 (accessed 03/05/2014)

Deen-Racsmány, Z. (2000, February). A Redistribution of Authority between the UN and
Regional Organisations in the Field of the Maintenance of Peace and Security. *Leiden*
Journal of International Law, Vol. 13 No 2, pp. 297–331.

Deutsche Welle. (2012, October 29). *UN envoy condemns Syria ceasefire failure.* Retrieved
from http://www.dw.de/un-envoy-condemns-syria-ceasefire-failure/a-16339906
(accessed 21/7/2014)

Deutsche Welle. (2012, October 29). *UN envoy condemns Syria ceasefire failure.* Retrieved
from http://www.dw.de/un-envoy-condemns-syria-ceasefire-failure/a-16339906
(accessed 20/7/2014)

Doyle, C. (2012, August 2). *Kofi Annan's Resignations Is No Suprise, His Syria Peace*
Undermined. Retrieved from Guardian:
http://www.guardian.co.uk/commentisfree/2012/aug/02/kofi-annan-resignation-
syria-peaceplan (accessed 03/05/2014)

Doyle, M. (2011, March 20). *The Folly of ProtectionIs: Intervention Against Qaddafi's Regime*
Legal and Legitimate? Retrieved from Foreign Affairs:
http://www.foreignaffairs.com/articles/67666/michael-w-doyle/the-folly-of-
protection (accessed 2/5/2014)

Ehtheshami, A. (2009). *Glabalization and Geopolitics in the Middle East.* London, United
Kingdom: Routledge.

Engle, E. (2014, April 2). A New Cold War? Cold Peace. Russia, Ukraine, and NATO... *St. Louis*
University Law Journal, pp. 1-90.

Evans, G., & Sahnoun, M. (2002). The Responsibility to Protect. *Foreign Affairs Vol. 81 No. 6,*
pp. 99-110.

Fabre, C. (2012). *Cosmopolitican War.* Oxford, United Kingdom: Oxford University Press.

Flick, U. (2011). *Introducing Research Methodology.* London, United Kingdom: SAGE
Publications.

Gause, G. I. (2011, July /August). *Why Middle East Studies Missed the Arab Spring.* Retrieved
from Foreign Affairs: http://www.foreignaffairs.com/articles/67932/f-gregory-gause-
iii/why-middle-east-studies-missed-the-arab-spring (accessed 20/5/2014)

Global Centre for the Responsibility to Protect. (2013, April 23). *UN Security Council*
Resolutions Referencing R2P. Retrieved from
http://s156658.gridserver.com/media/files/unsc-resolutions-and-statements-with-
r2p-table-as-of-may-2014.pdf (accessed 01/07/2014)

Goldstein, J., & Western, J. (2013, March 26). *R2P after Syria: To Save the Doctrine, Forget*
Regime Change. Retrieved from Foreign Affairs:

http://www.foreignaffairs.com/articles/67932/f-gregory-gause-iii/why-middle-east-studies-missed-the-arab-spring (accessed 20/5/2014)

Gwertzman, B. (2014, June 5). *How Iran Gains From Assad Victory.* Retrieved from Council on Foreign Relations: http://www.cfr.org/syria/iran-gains-assad-victory/p33064 (accessed 08/08/2014)

Haddad, B. (2012). *Business Networks in Syria: The Political Economy of Authoritarian Resilience.* Stanford, United States of America: Stanford University Press.

Hamilton, D. (2012, April 4). *Text of Annan's Six-Point Peace Plan for Syria.* Retrieved from Reuters: http://www.reuters.com/article/2012/04/04/us-syria-ceasefire-idUSBRE8330HJ20120404 (accessed 03/07/2014)

Hanano, A. (2012, December 11). *The Land of Topless Minarets and Headless Little Girls.* Retrieved from Foreign Policy: http://www.foreignpolicy.com/articles/2012/12/11/the_land_of_topless_minarets_a nd_headless_little_girls (accessed 03/06/2014)

Hart, H. (1961). *The Concept of Law.* Oxford, United Kingdom: Clarendon Press.

Hehir, A. (2010). *Humanitarian Intervention: An Introduction .* Basingstoke, United States: Palgrave McMillan.

Heydemann, S. (2013, October). Syria and the Future of Authoritarianims. *Journal of Democracy, Vol. 24, No. 4*, pp. 59-73.

Hinnebusch, R. (2002). The Foreign Policy of Syria. In R. Hinnebusch, & A. Etheshami, *The Foreign Policies of Middle East States* (pp. 141-167). London, United Kingdom: Lynne Rienner Publishers.

Hinnebusch, R. (2012, January). Syria: From 'authoritarian upgrading' to revolution? *International Affairs, Vol. 88 No.1*, p. 95.113.

Hough, P. (2004). *Understanding Global Security.* New York, United States: Routledge.

Hughes, G. (2014, July). Syria and the Peril of Proxy Warfare. *Smal Wars and Insurgencis Vol. 25, Issue 3*, pp. 522-538.

Hussein, T. (2013 , November 29). *A Brotherhood Vision for Syria.* Retrieved from The Majalla Magazine: http://www.majalla.com/eng/2013/11/article55247035 (accessed 6/7/2014)

Interfax. (2012, November 28). *Lavrov rules out Russia's involvement in armed conflict in Syria.* Retrieved from Russia beyond the headlines: http://rbth.co.uk/articles/2012/11/28/lavrov_rules_out_russias_involvement_in_ar med_conflict_in_syria_20489.html (accessed 27/07/2014)

Ismail, S. (2011, December). The Syrian Uprising: Imagining and Performing the Nation. *Studies in Ethnicity and Nationalism: Vol. 11, No. 3*, pp. 538-549.

Jadaliyya. (2014, January). Retrieved from http://syria.jadaliyya.com/ (accessed 03/07/14)

Jick, T. (1979, April). Mixing qualitative and quantitative methods: Triangulation in action. *Administrative Science Quarterly, Vol. 24 No.4*, pp. 602-611.

Kaplan, L. (2010). *NATO and the UN: a peculiar relationship.* Columbia, United States: University of Missouri Press.

Katz, M. (2013, June). Russia and the Conflict in Syria: Four Myths. *Middle East Policy Vol. 10, No. 2*, pp. 38-46.

Khashan, H. (2011, June). The view from Syria and Lebanon. *Middle East Quarterly, Vol. 18 No. 3*, pp. 25-30 .

Khoury, P. (1987). *Syria and the French Mandate: The Politics of Arab Nationalism 1920-1945.* London, United Kingdom: I.B. Tauris & Co.Ltd.

Kuperman, A. (2013). NATO's Intervention in Libya: A Humanitarian Success? In A. Hehir, & R. Murray, *Libya, the Responsibility to Protect and the Future of Humanitarian Intervention* (pp. 191-222). Basingstoke, United Kingdom: Palgrave McMillan.

Landis, J. (2012, March). The Syrian Uprising of 2011: Why the Assad Regime is likely to survive . *Middle East Poliy, Vol. Vol. 9 No. 1*, pp. 72- 84.

Laub, Z., & Masters, J. (2013, September 11). *Syria's Crisis and the Global Response.* Retrieved from Council on Foreign Relations : http://www.cfr.org/syria/syrias-crisis-global-response/p28402 (accessed 03/07/2014)

Lauterpacht, C. (2011, March). *Statement of the Gulf Cooperation Council, 7 March 2011.* Retrieved from Cambridge University Law Faculty Lauterpacht Centre: http://www.lcil.cam.ac.uk/sites/default/files/LCIL /documents/ arabspring /libya/Libya_13_AFP_Report.pdf (accessed 24/5/2014)

Lee, W. (2013, December). China's Stand on Humanitarian Intervention. *International Journal of China Studies Vol. 4, No. 3*, pp. 469-484.

Lehmann, C. (2013, September 30). *A Critical Review of Security Council Resolution 2118 (2013) on Syria.* Retrieved from NSBNC International: http://nsnbc.me/2013/09/30/security-council-resolution-syrias-chemical-weapons-un-balanced/ (accessed 12/7/2014)

MacFarquhar, N. (2011, November 12). *Arab League Votes to Suspend Syria Over Crackdown.* Retrieved from New York Times : http://www.nytimes.com/2011/11/13/world/middleeast/arab-league-votes-to-suspend-syria-over-its-crackdown-on-protesters.html?pagewanted=all&_r=0 (accessed 22/7/2014)

Mack, A., & Furlong, K. (2004). When Aspiration exceeds Capability: the UN and Conflict Prevention . In R. Price, & Z. Mark, *The United Nations and Global Security* (pp. 59-75). Basingstoke, United Kingdom: Palgrave McMillan.

Mamdani, M. (2010, March). Responsibility to Protect or Right to Punish? *Journal of Intervention and State Building Vol.4 No.1*, pp. 53-67.

Mason, A., & Wheeler, N. (1999). Realist Objections to Humanitarian Interventions. In B. Holden, *The Ethical Dimensions of Global Change* (p. 94.110). Basingstoke, United States: McMillan.

Nebehay, S. (2014, March 8). *List of suspected Syrian war criminals grows with atrocities: U.N.* Retrieved from Reuters: http://uk.reuters.com/article/2014/03/18/us-syria-crisis-warcrimes-idUKBREA2H0PH20140318 (accessed 02/07/2014)

Neep, D. (2012). *Occupying Syria under the French Mandate: Insurgency, Space and State Formation.* Cambridge, United Kingdom: Cambridge University Press.

Nickel, J. (1993, February). How human rights generate duties to protect and provide. *Human Rights Quarterly Vol. 15 No.1*, pp. 77-86.

O'Connell, M. (2012). Responsibility to Peace: A Critique on R2P. In P. Cunliffe, *Critical Perspectives on the Responsibility to Protect: Interrogating Theory and Practice* (pp. 71-84). London, United Kingdom: Routledge.

Parekh, B. (1997, January). Rethinking Humanitarian Intervention. *International Political Science Review Vol. 18 No. 1*, pp. 49-69.

Pawlak, J., & Croft, A. (2013, May 27). *EU failure will allow UK, France to arm Syrian rebels.* Retrieved from Reuters: http://www.reuters.com/article/2013/05/27/us-syria-crisis-eu-idUSBRE94Q09320130527 (accessed 08/07/2014)

Roberts, S. A. (2006). The United Nations and Humanitarian Interventions. In J. Welsh, *Humanitarian Interventions and International Relations* (pp. 71-98). Oxford, United Kingdom: Oxford University Press.

Ryan, C. (2012, April). *The New Arab Cold War and the Struggle for Syria.* Retrieved from Middle East Research and Information Project: http://www.merip.org/mer/mer262/new-arab-cold-war-struggle-syria (accessed 03/06/2014)

Schütte, R. (2012). Operationalizing the Reponsibility to Protect's "sharp end": Towards a No Footprint Approach? In D. Fiott, R. Zuber, & J. Koops, *Operationalizing the Responsibility to Protect: A Contribution to the Third Pillar Approach* (pp. 47-55). Brussels, Belgium: Madariage College of Europe Foundation;The Global Governance Institute;The International Coalition for the Responsibility to Protect.

Shapiro, J., & Charap, S. (2014, January 9). *Winning the Peace by Failing in Geneva.* Retrieved from Foreign Affairs: http://www.foreignaffairs.com/articles/140641/jeremy-shapiro-and-samuel-charap/winning-the-peace-by-failing-in-geneva (accessed 01/08/2014)

Shennib, G. (2014, February 14). *Libyan PM says government safe after army statement.* Retrieved from Reuters: http://uk.reuters.com/article/2014/02/14/uk-libya-crisis-idUKBREA1D0CO20140214 (accessed 4/7/2014)

Simon, S. (2013, July 16). *The Crisis in Syria: What are the Stakes for Syria's Neighbours.* Retrieved from Middle East Policy Council: http://www.mepc.org/hill-forums/crisis-syria-what-are-stakes-syrias-neighbors-0?transcript (accessed 03/07/2014)

Snidal, D. (2006). Rational Choice and International Relations. In B. Simmons, W. Carlsnaes, & T. Risse, *Handbook of International Relations* (pp. 73-95). London, United Kingdom: Sage Publications.

Stahn, C. (2007, January). Responsibility to Protect: Political Rhetiric or Emerging Legal Norm? *The American Journal of International Law Vol. 101 No.1*, pp. 99-120.

Stahn, C. (2013, October 3). *Syria, Security Resolution 2118 (2013) and Peace versus Justice: Two Steps Forward, One Step Back?* Retrieved from Blog of the European Journal of International Law: http://www.ejiltalk.org/syria-security-resolution-2118-2013-and-peace-versus-justice-two-steps-forward-one-step-back/ (accessed 23/6/2014)

Summer, T. (2013, September 20). *Syria Crisis: A Diplomatic Challenge for China.* Retrieved from Chatham House: https://www.chathamhouse.org/media/comment/view/194271 (accessed 21/07/2014)

Sun, Y. (2012, February 27). *Syria: What China Has Learned From its Libya Experience.* Retrieved from East West Centre: Asia Pacific Bulletin No. 152 : http://www.eastwestcenter.org/sites/default/files/private/apb152_1.pdf (accessed 08/08/2014)

Taylor, S. (2004, April). Researching educational policy and change in 'new times': using critical discourse analysis. *Journal of Education Policy, Vol.19 No4*, pp. 433-451.

Thakur, R. (2011, September 19). *Has R2P worked in Libya?* Retrieved from Canberra Times : http://www.canberratimes.com.au/federal-politics/editorial/has-r2p-worked-in-libya-20110918-1wqqb.html (accessed 22/5/2014)

Thomas, A. (2013, September). Pariah States and Sanctions: The Case of Syria. *Middle East Policy, Vol. 20 No. 3*, pp. 27-40.

Topham, J., & Tsukimori, O. (2014, June 7). *Huge Russia-China gas deal still leaves door open to Japan.* Retrieved from Reuters: http://uk.reuters.com/article/2014/06/07/uk-russia-japan-gas-idUKKBN0EI0V320140607 (accessed 06/07/2014)

Trading Economics. (2014, February). *Lebanon GDP Annual Growth Rate.* Retrieved from http://www.tradingeconomics.com/lebanon/gdp-growth-annual (accessed 11/08/2014)

Van Dam, N. (2011). *The Struggle for Power in Syria: Politics and Society under Assad and the Ba'ath Party.* London, United Kingdom: I.B. Tauris .

Vanderwalle, D. (2011, August 18). *Rebel Rivalries in Libya: Division and Disorder Undermine Libya's Opposition.* Retrieved from Foreign Affairs: http://www.foreignaffairs.com/articles/68198/dirk-vandewalle/rebel-rivalries-in-libya (accessed 6/7/2014)

Weiss, T. (2004). The Sunset of Humanitarian Intervention? The Responsibility to Protect in a Unipolar Era. *Security Dialogue Vol. 35*, pp. 135-153.

Weiss, T. (2007, April). *Humanitarian intervention: ideas in action.* Cambridge, United Kingdom: Polity.

Welsh, J. (2004). *Humanitarian Intervention and International Relations.* Oxford, United Kingdom: Oxford University Press.

Welsh, J. (2011, September). Civilian Protection in Libya: Putting Coercion and Controversy Back into R2P. *Ethics and International Affairs Vol.25 Issue 03*, pp. 255-262.

West's Encyclopedia of American Law. (2008). *Jus Cogens.* Retrieved from Legal Dictionary Online: http://legal-dictionary.thefreedictionary.com/Jus+Cogens (accessed 17/6/2014)

Wheeler, N. (2000). *Saving Strangers: Humanitarian Intervention in International Society.* Oxford, Great Britain: Oxford University Press.

Williams, P. (2011, February). The Road to Humanitarian War in Libya. *Global Responsibilty to Protect, Vol.3, Issue 2*, pp. 248-259.

Winnet, R. (2013, August 29). *Syria Crisis: No to war, blow to Cameron.* Retrieved from The Telegraph: http://www.telegraph.co.uk/news/worldnews/middleeast/syria/10275158/Syria-crisis-No-to-war-blow-to-Cameron.html (accessed 02/07/2014)

Woodhouse, T., & Ramsbotham, O. (1998). Peacekeeping and Humanitian Intervention in Post-War Conflicts. In T. Woodhouse, R. Bruce, & M. Dando, *Peakeeping and Peacemaking: Towards Effective Intervention in Post-Cold War Conflicts* (pp. 39-74). Basingstoke, United Kingdom: Palgrave Macmillan.

Yacoubian, M. (2006, November 9). *Syria's Role in Lebanon.* Retrieved from United States Institute for Peace: http://www.usip.org/publications/syrias-role-in-lebanon (accessed 06/08/2014)

Zacher, M. (2004). The Conundrums of International Power Sharing: The Politics of the Security Council . In R. Price, & M. Zacher, *The United Nations and Global Security* (pp. 211-227). Basingstoke, United Kingdom: Palgrave McMillan.